Accidental City

Accic

ental

City

Accidental City

THE TRANSFORMATION OF TORONTO

Robert Fulford

A Peter Davison Book

HOUGHTON MIFFLIN COMPANY

BOSTON · NEW YORK · 1996

For information about permission to reproduce
selections from this book, write to Permissions,
Houghton Mifflin Company,
215 Park Avenue South,
New York, NY 10003.

First published:
Canada: Macfarlane Walter & Ross, 1995

CIP data is available.
ISBN 0-395-77307-5

Printed in Canada

10 9 8 7 6 5 4 3 2 1

For Frances Fulford, who brought me to Toronto in 1932

Photography by Steven Evans

Contents

Toronto

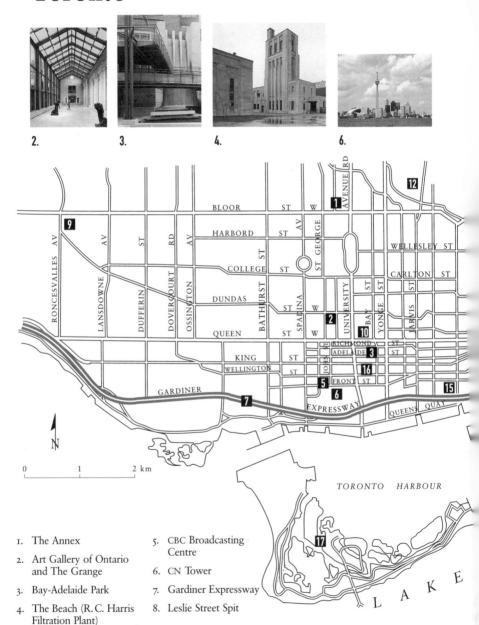

2.   3.   4.   6.

TORONTO HARBOUR

LAKE

1. The Annex

2. Art Gallery of Ontario and The Grange

3. Bay-Adelaide Park

4. The Beach (R. C. Harris Filtration Plant)

5. CBC Broadcasting Centre

6. CN Tower

7. Gardiner Expressway

8. Leslie Street Spit

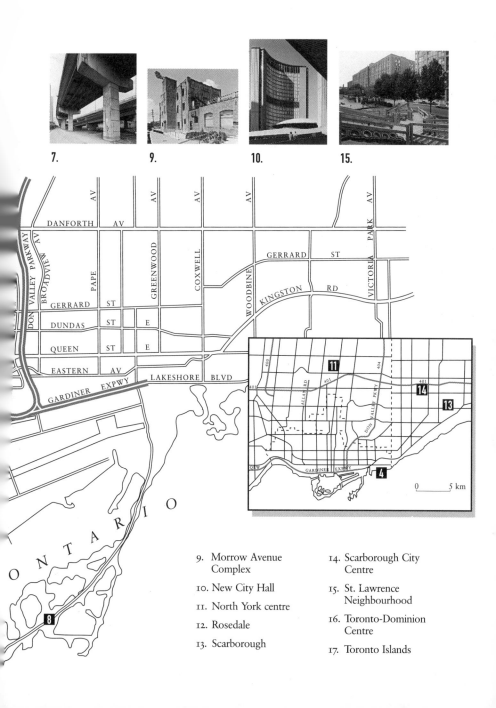

7. **9.** **10.** **15.**

I

Going Public

THE GREAT CRITIC Northrop Frye, an ornament of the city for half a century, once called Toronto a good place to mind your own business. Thirty or forty years ago, the most obvious quality of Toronto was reticence, which many mistook for a virtue. Toronto was a city of silence, a private city, where all the best meals were eaten at home and no one noticed the absence of street life and public spaces. Sidewalk cafés were illegal, and there were no festivals. The idea of public art was still exotic and alien. The 1907 Lord's Day Act, which forbade almost all public activity on Sunday except churchgoing, was obeyed with a dedication that visitors thought excessive. Many accomplished and admirable people lived in Toronto, scrupulously minding their own business, but the city itself denied that it had an identity worth exhibiting.

In the 1950s, the grandest architectural space in Toronto was a place of passage rather than destination, the great hall in Union Station. The grandest boulevard, University Avenue, was a double row of faceless tombstones that marched glumly northward from Front Street until finally turning into something bearing the absurd name Avenue Road, which sounds like an identity crisis with pavement. Toronto's most famous painters, the Group of Seven, ignored their city (the young Lawren Harris was the one exception) and turned to the northern wilderness for inspiration. In fiction, Toronto barely existed. The often unnamed version of it depicted in Morley Callaghan's sad and lovely novels registers as a collection of villages and small towns, self-contained, unknown to each other.

Wyndham Lewis, the English writer and painter, spent several miserable years in Toronto in the 1940s and called it "a sanctimonious ice-box ... this bush-metropolis of the Orange Lodges." A few years later, back in England, he wrote *Self Condemned*, a novel in which wartime Toronto is disguised as charmless and unwelcoming Momaco. Even those who were raised in the Toronto elite found their native city hard to love. The poet Anne Wilkinson, who grew up in Rosedale as part of the great Osler clan, considered Toronto "the home of righteous mediocrity." On May 11, 1948, she wrote in her diary: "A true test of love for a Torontonian: If you can walk down Yonge St. with your beloved and still think man's world is a thing of beauty, it's love. I can't."

This mute, inward-turned metropolis was the city I knew as a child and a young man, from the Depression to the 1960s. The last thirty years have transformed it, spiritually as well as physically. The dream-life of Toronto, its civic ambition, has changed profoundly. In Toronto, city-building has become an art of public revelation rather than private expression. Toronto is a private city that finally became public, and gradually acquired a desire to be seen and understood. Slowly, often by accident, sometimes with reluctance, it has learned to disclose itself.

The significant moment of change can be precisely dated: Monday, September 13, 1965, opening day at the New City Hall and Nathan Phillips Square, both designed by the Finnish architect Viljo Revell. At the time, it was the big new municipal building, with its curved towers embracing an oyster-shaped council chamber, that commanded attention. It was a huge sculpture cast in concrete, a romantic departure from the cool geometry of modernism that dominated architecture in the western world and would continue to dominate downtown Toronto. The large public square to the south appeared incidental and was not much discussed, but it turned out to be a more radical departure than the building itself.

It was, unabashedly, a civic space, open to an infinity of uses. This was a break with the past, something new for Toronto, a stage where the people could act out their beliefs and understand themselves as citizens rather than consumers and workers. As an idea it was ancient. In *The City Assembled*, Spiro Kostof quotes a fourteenth-century French writer's remark that "through piazzas the condition of man in this world can be discovered." Kostof calls this a tribute to the universal human need for public space: "Cities of every age have seen fit to make provision for open places that would promote social encounters and serve the conduct of public affairs." With the creation of Nathan Phillips Square, Toronto began joining itself to that tradition.

THIS MAJOR STEP in the evolution of Toronto's civic consciousness now seems to have been almost inevitable. Clearly, Nathan Phillips Square, or something like it, had to happen. But in fact, Toronto stumbled toward that epiphany in 1965 – stumbled, fell from the path, stopped dead several times, all but gave up. It took fifty-four years to create the city's first piazza.

It began as a proposal outlined in 1911 by John M. Lyle, a stylish and successful Toronto architect of the day. Working on a commission for the Civic Improvement Committee, Lyle proposed a great square on the north side of Queen Street, between the Old City Hall and the law courts in Osgoode Hall. He wasn't thinking of a headquarters for local government: Edward J. Lennox's noble Romanesque Revival building was only twelve years old, and serving very well as the City Hall. What Lyle wanted was a statement of civic grandeur. Having trained at the Ecole des Beaux-Arts in Paris, he embraced the "City Beautiful" movement, whose propaganda led to Neo-Classical squares across the United States. He outlined a generous open space surrounded by federal and local offices (a registry office was in fact built, and later demolished). This plaza would look down a grand new street, Federal Avenue, running from Queen to Union Station on Front Street – though the station of today wasn't built until a few years later, with Lyle one of the architects.

Lyle's Federal Avenue never came into being, but the idea of the square was lodged in the local imagination, a fantasy of a possible future. Alfred Chapman, the architect of the Princes' Gates at the Canadian National Exhibition (and later of the Royal Ontario Museum and Holy Blossom Temple) drew up another ambitious plan for the same space in 1927. Two years later the city planning commission proposed that a single building dominate the site. The Depression and the Second World War put these ideas aside, but in 1946 they came to life again. In a plebiscite, the voters agreed to buy most of the land on which Lyle had proposed to place the square. By 1951 city council agreed to build a new city hall.

Who would design it? It would be a coup for the firm chosen, and most of the prominent architects of the city quietly put themselves forward. The politicians, unable to decide and unwilling to make enemies, devised what they imagined would be a fruitful and agreeable compromise. In 1953 they commissioned three firms to work together – Mathers & Haldenby, Marani & Morris, and Shore & Moffat. The first two were considered highly conservative, the favourites of insurance companies; the third was thought to be more in tune with up-to-date thinking. In 1955 this consortium presented a drawing (made by a professional renderer, imported from New York for the purpose) of their proposed building. It was austere and characterless, much like the insurance buildings then proliferating on Bloor Street. When published in the newspapers, it attracted few supporters and many detractors. Architecture students at the University of Toronto campaigned against it. That year, when a money bill to pay for the city hall was put on the municipal ballot, the voters defeated it. A year later, in 1956, the voters accepted the idea of a city hall in another plebiscite; but clearly they had rejected the design they had been shown.

The city still had a contract with the three architectural firms; to choose a fourth might have involved lawsuits, and certainly would have created trouble with the Ontario Association of Architects, which was carefully monitoring the process on behalf of the profession. Mayor Nathan Phillips, who had not liked the design any more than the voters did, looked for another approach. The idea presented to him, a competition, would somehow transcend the city's obligations to the three architectural firms (who were paid for their drawing) and would free the mayor from having to choose one kind of architecture over another. The city-planning commissioner, Matthew Lawson, favoured a competition open to the whole world. So did Eric Arthur, an architect and teacher who had for many years been serving as a kind of architectural conscience to the city.

Not everyone liked the idea. Many Canadian architects thought that this important building should be the work of a Canadian. Would a foreigner, with foreign ideas, be acceptable to the city? The Toronto *Telegram* quoted the bizarre objection of Forsey Page, of the firm Page & Steele: "What would happen if the Chinese Communists ... submitted the most dramatic design?" But city council finally decided on an international competition, with an international panel of architects as judges: Sir William Holford from London, Ned Pratt from Vancouver, Ernesto Rogers from Milan, Gordon Stephenson from the University of Toronto, and Eero Saarinen from Bloomfield Hills, Michigan. Eric Arthur was appointed professional adviser and non-voting chairman.

In September, 1957, council approved the terms of the competition, and from that point things moved at remarkable speed. A booklet went out around the world describing the site and the city, with some emphasis on the square: "The Corporation sees the Square fulfilling the function of many ancient, and some more recent public spaces.... The Square will sometimes be used as a place of public assembly as on occasions of national rejoicing." Submissions had to be in by April 18, 1958, less than seven months away.

The response astonished everyone: 510 models with accompanying drawings arrived in Toronto from forty-two countries. There were high-rise slabs, buildings raised on stilts, pyramids, structures in the form of spirals, buildings shaped around inner courtyards. There were proposals from well-known architects, such as I. M. Pei, and from architects never heard of before or since. There was one remarkable plan from John Andrews of Australia, who didn't win but came to Canada as a result of the competition and later designed Scarborough College as a brutalist megastructure for the University of Toronto.

All entries were assigned numbers and shown anonymously to the judges; Eric Arthur held sealed envelopes naming each architect, to be opened when eight finalists were chosen. He laid out the models in a huge building on the Canadian National Exhibition grounds and waited for the judges to arrive. Four of them came on time: Holford, Pratt, Rogers, and Stephenson. One, Saarinen, arrived a day and half late, and without much in the way of a convincing apology. As Arthur told the story later, the others found this cavalier behaviour irritating; perhaps they saw it as an arrogant reminder that Saarinen was at that moment the most famous and successful member of the panel, and therefore the busiest. What happened next was far more irritating. Saarinen asked what they had been doing, and they told him they had eliminated many of the obvious non-starters. He then spoke the most offensive sentence he could have uttered: "Show me your discards." They sighed, but indulged him – and in the designs they had discarded he found Viljo Revell's submission, which looked a little like one of Saarinen's own buildings. In the end, Saarinen persuaded a majority of his fellow judges that it should not only be a finalist but also the winner. It is not recorded whether anyone expressed annoyance or astonishment when all of them learned that the architect was, like Saarinen, Finnish.

Revell's design was published on September 26, 1958, to general astonishment. Those who admired modern architecture thought it highly promising, even delightful, certainly audacious. Those suspicious of modern architecture regarded it as outlandish. The usual outrage spattered the letters columns of the papers. "Two boomerangs over half a grapefruit" said one letter to the editor. "A couple of pieces of old broken sewer pipe" said another. Nevertheless, the city signed a contract with Revell in 1958, and the first sod was turned in November, 1961.

The building itself profoundly influenced the city without having any notable effect on the history of architecture. No one ever imitated Revell's design; for all its power as an image, it has never been taken as a model by younger architects. But it transformed Toronto by cracking open the city's prejudices about how buildings should look; the public idea of what was acceptable in architecture seemed to change overnight. The gray conservatism of the Bloor Street insurance buildings and the institutionalized anonymity of University Avenue were no longer the city's inevitable styles. Modern architecture suddenly became legitimate and respectable. It was one of those rare occasions when a city government provided genuine leadership in design.

Thirty years later, Revell's building performs best as an icon, an image of genial modernity. He clearly saw himself as a form-giver rather than a builder of efficient spaces. No one has ever claimed that the offices of the City Hall work especially well; many of them are inconvenient to use, and difficult to heat and cool. The two big interior spaces, the council chamber and the library, achieve a delicate combination of intimacy and grandeur.

But the square is the real triumph. Since opening day, it has been the great living room of Toronto, the place where citizens gather to hold public meetings, to celebrate triumphs, to mourn lost heroes like John Lennon or welcome great figures like Nelson Mandela. It quickly became a genuine town square, just as John Lyle imagined in 1911 and the framers of the competition asked in 1957. Ron Thom, the architect best known in Toronto for designing Massey College, wrote in *Canadian Architect*: "It has spawned an entirely different sort of life at the core. Public interest has been awakened to such an extent that careful development has become a political concern." As Thom predicted, it also affected the future development of the land surrounding it. In later years Nathan Phillips Square spread, westward to the pedestrian spaces around Osgoode Hall and northeast to Trinity Square, designed by the Thom Partnership.

The reflecting pool that turns into a skating rink in winter has been a long-term success, as have the arches over it that echo the curved shapes of the buildings. The gigantic elevated walkway that Revell put around the square remains controversial. Many find it constricting, and imagine a day when it will be torn down to create a more expansive public space. There are others who think, as I do, that it was a masterstroke that defines the space visually, giving it a firm identity while leaving it open to everyone who wants to wander through. In their book *Toronto Observed* (1986), William Dendy and William Kilbourn called Nathan Phillips Square "one of the few civic plazas created in a modern city to capture the hearts of the citizens." They believed that the city council of 1958 almost certainly envisioned a much more formal space, calmer and duller. "It is to Viljo Revell and his humanistic concept of ancient and modern city forms, and of urban life itself, that Toronto owes the success of its civic square. Without it the building would have been forever incomplete."

AT THE OPENING CEREMONIES, Prime Minister Lester B. Pearson said of the New City Hall: "It is an edifice as modern as tomorrow – as modern as the day after tomorrow." At that moment, Pearson himself was helping to change Toronto's tomorrow. His government was revising the immigration rules, eliminating the racial barriers that had sharply limited the number of non-whites admitted to Canada. The completion of the New City Hall roughly coincided with this change, which affected Toronto more than any other part of Canada.

Like so many good things in Toronto, the design of the first great square was the work of immigrants. Eric Arthur was a New Zealander who arrived by way of Liverpool. Matthew Lawson was British, as were most of the senior members of his city-planning staff. And it was a Finnish architect's belief in urban life that gave shape to generations of dreams and provided the city's focal point. This is where the new Toronto was born, and many of the monuments of post-1965 Toronto have been echoes of Revell's bold vision, or extensions of it, or responses to it. We can see some of that same expansive spirit in Ontario Place, the Metropolitan Toronto Central Reference Library, the CN Tower, the Eaton Centre, the Bay-Adelaide Park, the atrium in BCE Place, the St. Lawrence Neighbourhood, and the ambitious public squares in Scarborough and Mississauga. At the same time, the story of post-1965 Toronto building is by no means an undiluted triumph: there have been failures as well, unhappy accidents, such as the CBC Broadcasting Centre and the North York centre.

THE INFLUENCE of the New City Hall is in some cases oblique, but one magnificent Toronto monument came into being as a direct result: the Henry Moore Sculpture Centre at the Art Gallery of Ontario (AGO), the most striking permanent art exhibit in eastern Canada, where visitors walk among gigantic lumps of plaster on which a master imposed his vision. It's the most important public collection of Henry Moore's work anywhere, and the largest single gift in the history of Canadian museums – some 900 Moore items, including 139 sculptures, most of them donations from Moore himself. It emerged, through a series of happy accidents, from a public argument that Viljo Revell inadvertently set in motion.

In 1964, when his City Hall was being finished, Revell decided that the square should have a large sculpture by Moore, whom he greatly admired. He visited Moore at his studio in Much Hadham, Hertfordshire, and together they selected a working model, *Three-Way Piece No. 2 (The Archer)*. They agreed that, when enlarged and cast in bronze, it would complement the form of Revell's building. On the day after their meeting, Revell died of a heart attack in Helsinki. His brief visit to Much Hadham eventually ignited one of the great Toronto controversies of the day, put art at the centre of local politics, and had a lasting influence on city government.

Revell had not discussed his idea for a sculpture with city council, and certainly hadn't obtained official backing for it. But with Revell dead, Moore seems to have mistakenly assumed that the choice he and Revell had made was final. Moore soon got in touch with Toronto to inquire about preparing the bronze casting and placing it. And then there was the matter of his fee.

When this became known in Toronto, it quickly divided city council. Mayor Philip Givens, a lawyer who dreamt of making Toronto sophisticated and up-to-date, favoured buying the sculpture. William Dennison, his opponent in the election to be held in a few months, opposed it. Dennison was an unusual man, a speech therapist who had invented a cure for stammering that brought patients from all over the continent and an amateur bee-keeper who rushed to the scene with his equipment whenever a swarm of unwanted bees suddenly appeared in some frightened citizen's backyard. On the subject of art, however, he was an old-fashioned Torontonian. He thought Moore's work highbrow and elitist. "Culture should be for the broad mass of people as well as for the selected few," he said. "Standards of art should be guided basically by what the most people enjoy...."

Much of Toronto took sides, and various aldermen offered the opinion that the cost ($123,000, which Moore later reduced to $100,000) was outrageous. Givens managed to buy *The Archer* with money raised privately, and installed it on the square. At the unveiling, on the evening of October 27, 1966, Eric Arthur – who chaired the City Hall art committee as well as the building competition – said that the installation was a triumph for art and for the future of the city. "The philistines," he said, "have retired in disorder." The reviews in the newspapers were admiring. Some public resentment lingered, expressed occasion-ally in vandalism; in 1967 someone spray-painted a message on the sculpture: "Givens is a bumb [sic] he should have spent it on slums." But the sculpture quickly became a much-photographed, much-discussed landmark, always called "the Henry Moore," rather than *The Archer* – as in the title of Murray McLauchlan's song, "Down by the Henry Moore."

Still, the city's affection didn't produce enough votes for Givens. While bringing the Moore to Toronto, Givens said, "Even if I lose the election over this, I don't care. I've gotta do what I think is right." Dennison won, and Givens retired from city politics. He believed that he lost because he supported the Moore, and he's always insisted that he's glad he did. In 1994 Givens remembered the tangled feelings of the voters: "I went out and raised the dough [from a dozen anonymous donors] and they held it against me...we could never get it through the heads of the people of Toronto that it cost them nothing."

That election reconfigured local politics, by providing a negative focus for the emerging anti-development, save-the-neighbourhoods movement. Dennison, who had originally joined city council as a socialist, took an unexpected turn in the mayor's office: he became the great friend of big property developers. The anti-development politicians and their supporters, who would eventually elect David Crombie and then John Sewell as mayor, formed an alliance against Dennison and the members of council who voted with him, now called "the old guard." The reform movement established the ground rules for Toronto politics in the 1970s. Had Givens remained mayor for two or three terms, the political landscape almost certainly would have taken a different shape.

The battle over *The Archer* also forged an emotional connection between Moore and Toronto. In the mid-1960s, moving through his seventh decade, he was thinking about the eventual disposition of the many sculptures he owned, especially the large original plasters from which his major bronze pieces had been cast. He assumed that the Tate Gallery in London would build a wing to house his work, and some directors of the Tate apparently encouraged that belief. Eventually, however, they resisted the idea – as did many younger English sculptors, who expressed their views in a famous letter to the *Times* of London that left Moore feeling mortified and unappreciated.

In Moore's conversations with various Toronto friends, including the financier Sam Zacks, the idea of a Moore donation to Toronto came up. Zacks, a major benefactor of the Art Gallery of Ontario, and William Withrow, the director, came away from these conversations with the belief that Toronto might acquire a great deal of Moore's work if it provided the right setting. To the Torontonians, their city seemed the natural home for a Moore gallery. Toronto collectors had been buying his work long before the New City Hall, and from its beginnings the AGO had taken a special interest in British art.

The man who helped develop the later phases of this policy was one of the most remarkable figures in the British art establishment, Anthony Blunt. In 1947 the director of the Art Gallery,

Martin Baldwin, retained him as a London representative, at a fee of £700 a year. As a renowned scholar, as director of the Courtauld Institute, and as curator of the Queen's art collection, Blunt was well placed to identify items that Toronto might acquire. For about two decades he provided advice on purchases, including Tintoretto's *Christ Washing His Disciples' Feet* in 1959. He cabled from London: ANY CHANCE OF INTEREST-ING YOU IN SUPERB TINTORETTO "X" THOUSAND POUNDS STOP SUBJECT CHRIST WASHING APOSTLES FEET REPRODUCED BERCKEN PLATE 28. The figure turned out to be $100,000, which the gallery raised by drawing a graph of tiny squares over a reproduction of the painting and then asking the public to buy it at $10 a square.

Blunt's position as London representative was eliminated in the 1960s, after the gallery developed its own professional staff, but it produced a *frisson* of retrospective excitement in 1979. That was the year the British government revealed that Blunt, as a member of the British secret service, had been a spy for the Soviet Union. At age seventy-two he was stripped of his knight-hood and his royal assignment, though not prosecuted. "This was a case of political conscience against loyalty to country," he said of his service to the USSR. "I chose conscience." He spoke as if treason was the mark of an elevated soul.

It was Blunt who suggested that the gallery acquire its first major Henry Moore, *Warrior with Shield*. In the 1960s Toronto's interest in British art was slowly giving way to a fascination with the Abstract Expressionists of New York, but interest in British culture was still lively. And Moore's reputation was at its height. The AGO, everyone agreed, would make an ideal setting for a permanent celebration of the most admired English artist of the century. After the first discussions in Toronto, Withrow and Zacks talked to Moore several times. On one occasion they took the premier of Ontario, John Robarts, to England so that he could provide the province's blessing and convince Moore of their seriousness. Still, both Moore and the gallery remained tentative and a little coy, each wondering what the other was willing to offer.

In 1969 a young Toronto scholar, Alan Wilkinson, happened to be working on a doctoral thesis on Moore's drawings at the Courtauld Institute in London. Withrow engaged him to work part-time as, in Withrow's phrase, "our man at Much Hadham." It was his job to discover what would satisfy Moore and convey to Moore what Toronto was planning, all the while subtly suggesting ways in which Moore's gift might be enlarged. In the end Moore became not only the donor but also the architect of his own memorial. As Wilkinson has said: "The big Moore gallery was completely his design." He decided on the shape (a double square) and the size, including the height – about eighteen feet, twice the height of the tallest sculpture he was planning to donate. In a field at Much Hadham, Moore and Wilkinson paced off the dimensions and put down logs to indicate the corners. Moore dictated the precise off-white shade of the walls and insisted on soft natural light from above, so that the sculptures could be seen for themselves and never as silhouettes on the walls; he didn't like silhouettes.

Moore visited Toronto several times to check on progress, and spent two weeks at the gallery in the fall of 1974, supervising the installation. He also helped choose, and place, the gigantic *Large Two Forms*, which sits on the sidewalk on Dundas Street, announcing the Moore Centre's presence – a spectacular example of the new fashion for public art that took hold in Toronto in the decade after the New City Hall opening.

At first there were more than twenty-five sculptures in the main room, perhaps because Moore couldn't bear to consign more of them to the storerooms. The space was crowded to the point of claustrophobia, but within a year Wilkinson winnowed the number down to a more comfortable eighteen, which is what we can see there now. Wilkinson had joined the AGO's permanent staff after returning from England, and over two decades he acquired enough sculpture to make the space beside the Moore Centre into a coherent display of Moore's contemporaries, from Barbara Hepworth to Alberto Giacometti. Building on Moore's gift, he created something unique in Canada and uncommon elsewhere – a display of the context in which major European art was made. None of this could have happened if Revell had not designed the City Hall and then decided it needed a Henry Moore. Wilkinson was still at work on this project in 1994 when he and his vast knowledge were more or less discarded by Glenn Lowry, the AGO director, who favoured new management techniques and wanted an up-to-date staff. A month after firing Wilkinson, Lowry himself resigned to become director of the Museum of Modern Art in New York.

ACCIDENTS OFTEN HAPPEN in city building, and if a city is fortunate its accidents express the feelings and needs of the citizens; perhaps the story of Toronto in the last thirty years is a story, more than anything else, of happier-than-usual accidents, like the Moore Centre. The result of these events has been the creation of a civic mood that both welcomes newcomers and nourishes the lives of people born here.

What quality sets one city apart from others? That question has been discussed since the first great cities were built in antiquity. Today the condition of life in the industrial world gives it a fresh urgency. Modern society lives under a curse of uniformity. Technology and marketing conspire to standardize much of what surrounds us, from television programs to cars. This ocean of sameness offends the central humanist belief that each of us is unique. Cities, if designed with skill and imagination, can help us elude the tyranny of uniformity. Living in a city with a unique character can give life a knowable context and help us understand ourselves as individuals. The built city can join its citizens together or push them apart, hide our collective memories or reveal them, encourage our best instincts or our worst. In a pluralistic society that lacks common beliefs, public physical structures provide an experience we all share, a common theatre of memories.

A successful city fulfills itself not by master plans but through an attentiveness to the processes that have created it and an awareness of its possibilities. It achieves a heightened identity by giving form to memory and providing space for new life. Toronto doesn't always succeed in distinguishing itself from similar places. At times it seems to be no more than the nicest city in the American League, an imitation U.S. metropolis with a cheaper dollar and less crime. But under examination it turns out to have a style of its own, a style worth understanding and cherishing. The architect-theorist George Baird once wrote that for Toronto "the way forward will lie in seizing the forms of rhetoric and commerce themselves for symbolic representations, the precise meaning of which we will not be able to predict in advance." It is a difficult, rewarding, sometimes rancorous process. Toronto has been living it since 1965.

2

The View from the CN Tower

IT IS THE unlikely symbol of the city's collective achievements, the absurd embodiment of Toronto dreams, the most powerful public work of art in Canada. There is no avoiding it. If you approach the city by car, boat, or plane, what you see first is that thick concrete pencil pushed through a gleaming steel donut into the clouds. Within the city, it never leaves us: walking or driving, we glimpse its looming phallic shape everywhere, intruding on hundreds of leafy old streets, the only landmark visible above the rooftops. Even indoors, it's omnipresent, Toronto's logo on everything from postcards to television screens.

Judged against most of the towers built around the world in recent decades, from Seattle to Moscow, the CN Tower looks elegant and confident. At times it's even magical. When a low-level cloud appears, the pod and the missile-like point above seem to float free of the base, as if bringing visitors from another planet. The architect Jack Diamond has identified the best place to see it: stand on the northeast corner of Bay and King and look southwest through Ludwig Mies van der Rohe's T-D Centre. Two black skyscrapers frame the tower, creating an accidental abstract sculpture that embodies all the power and arrogance of modernist design.

Not everyone is happy with the CN Tower. Like an aggressive old acquaintance who sometimes grows tiresome but never disappears, it remains lodged in our lives. It recalls Guy de

Maupassant's remark: "I like to lunch at the Eiffel Tower, because that's the only place in Paris where I can't see the Eiffel Tower." Like the Eiffel Tower, the CN Tower used the most sophisticated engineering of its time mainly to demonstrate its own importance: it's an exercise in self-assertion, a spectacular case of tower for tower's sake. Yet in a sense it's an altogether appropriate emblem for the Toronto that has been recreated during the last thirty years.

Toronto people feel ambivalent about it, as we feel ambivalent about much of what has been built around us. By tradition, Torontonians silently agree that to declare oneself proud of the city is to step dangerously close to gaucherie. Once I was astonished to hear myself utter the words "My beloved Toronto" on a radio program. Those words were not false: like the fortunate partner in a happy marriage, I love Toronto and find my love steadily growing. But that sort of phrase is rarely uttered, by me or anyone else. A defensive ambivalence is our local style, bred in the bone of born Torontonians, quickly adopted as protective colouration by newcomers. We understand that we have built a diverse and densely international city on top of the old British metropolis that was created in the nineteenth century and the first half of the twentieth. At the same time, we wonder whether we haven't made some gigantic mistake in building so much, so high, so fast.

If the CN Tower comes up in conversation with visitors, local people may mention that it's the tallest building (or "freestanding structure") on the planet but will quickly add that they themselves have never bothered to ride the elevator up to the observation platform. Few Torontonians have a kind word to say about the tower, but it is one structure that speaks eloquently of the place and time in which it was built. In the 1970s the city was struggling to shake off the dowdy self-image that was part of its heritage as a colonial city perpetually living in someone else's shadow: too British to be American, too American to be British, and too cosmopolitan to be properly Canadian. But we were changing. The New City Hall had opened fresh possibilities. As the tower was being planned, Torontonians were starting to consider, with shy pleasure, the novel idea that their city might be attractive, even enviable. American magazine articles and TV documentaries caressed Toronto's civic ego by describing "the city that works," a place that had escaped the gravest urban problems. At that happy moment, the tower reinforced local exuberance and asserted the city's claim to even more attention.

Given Toronto's role in Canada and the world, a communications tower makes a felicitous symbol. Toronto has for a long while been the centre of mass media and publishing in Canada, and over the years has asserted some international leadership in cable-television and cellular phones. Torontonians are devoted connoisseurs of mass culture, maybe the most enthusiastic moviegoers in the western world, certainly the pioneers of the multi-channel universe: for some years, before satellites and cable, Toronto watched seven TV networks, more than any other city in the world. It was not an accident that the most often quoted theorist of mass media, Marshall McLuhan, developed his ideas at the University of Toronto.

Like many of the most significant landmarks of Toronto, the CN Tower is linked in the public mind to no individual designer or business executive. In Toronto, some of the most imposing structures bear no familiar signatures: they're the work of people whose names are little known or not known at all. This is true, for instance, of another powerful landmark, the SkyDome, which symbolized the paper wealth of 1980s Toronto, just as the CN Tower symbolized the city's thrusting ambition of the 1970s. The SkyDome's architect is mentioned in public no more often than the man who designed the CN Tower. In the SkyDome's case, that's just as well. However efficiently it functions as a ball park, it's a lumpy and unlovable element in the cityscape, sitting on the edge of downtown like a gigantic toadstool – and the monstrous cartoon-sculptures made by the city's most admired artist, Michael Snow, do nothing to make it more agreeable.

The creators of the highway system that defines the local geography are equally obscure. In Toronto the most crucial planning decisions are usually made by traffic engineers, with effects that do not become clear to the citizens until later. Aside from Lake Ontario, three crucial lines give Toronto its shape, all of them expressways built in the 1950s and the 1960s – Highway 401, whose sixteen lanes race across the top of the city; the Don Valley Parkway, which runs down the river valley at the east side of downtown; and the Gardiner Expressway, a 1950s planning mistake so horrendous that it may take another century to fix. The commercial core of Toronto contains a remarkable structure that also appears to have no author: the vast empire of shopping malls and tunnels beneath the downtown towers. Many cities have tunnels connecting the railway station with two or three hotels or office buildings, but the Toronto system is by far the most extensive in the world, its ten kilometres linking the subways and the railroad with skyscrapers, hotels, and local government. Where the CN Tower presents the vertical and blatant image of Toronto commerce, the underground city registers as a hidden equivalent. It's become a kind of alternative city beneath the real one, the creation of mainly anonymous forces.

ROLAND BARTHES CLAIMED that the Eiffel Tower changed everyone's understanding of Paris: the visitor who ascends it becomes part of the tower rather than part of the city, and Paris itself turns into an object for contemplation. A visit to the restaurant that revolves within the pod of the CN Tower has an even more radical effect. From 370 metres in the air, Toronto becomes a different place. The tower, working a kind of technological magic, forces us to adopt its own colossal sense of scale. We see Toronto as the tower sees it.

The view from some lesser perch, like the rooftop bar of the Park Plaza Hotel, encourages warm and comfortable ideas about the city – it looks greener than we might have thought, splendidly varied, altogether attractive. If we think kindly of Toronto, the Plaza roof confirms our opinions. The view from the CN Tower has a different effect. It reduces the presence of nature (the river valleys vanish from view) and amplifies the intimidating strength of communications systems by placing the naked evidence of them at our feet. The tower itself, a textbook example of streamlined modern design, with all its TV and radio antennae carefully hidden, seems to sit in harsh judgment on the chaotic city beneath it. Height becomes a kind of rhetorical power, forcing a new look at the city. It redraws our local map, rewrites our memories of Toronto. It obliterates history, nature, and even the logic of the streets.

The restaurant scans the city in seventy-two minutes. As it begins to revolve, starting at the lake, Toronto Island – with its big park, yacht clubs, and forty-year-old political controversy – is reduced to miniature size, the passionately defended homes of its residents barely discernible. On the mainland, the first surprise is Fort York, that beleaguered survivor of the War of 1812. It is only a few blocks to the west, but from the tower it loses its identity. It doesn't look like a fort at all, just some brownish lumps, far less impressive than the railroad tracks that spread westward from the tower's foot. Close by, the powerful, self-assertive Gardiner Expressway suddenly looks rickety on its matchstick legs. From there, if we follow Bathurst Street and Spadina Avenue north with our eyes, past Bloor Street, we can pick out the Annex and then, to the east, Rosedale – two old Toronto districts that have developed the rich identity of small European principalities.

Both of them emerge anonymously from history, linked to no particular architect, builder, or mansion-owner. The Annex has the more checkered past. In the late 1880s, the leaders of prosperous Toronto, like Timothy Eaton and Edmund Walker, began to fill it with Queen Anne and Romanesque Revival houses, built of pink sandstone and brick. While respecting the harmony of the streetscape, the builders indulged in such a multitude of bay windows, turrets, eccentric stonework and terra-cotta that a walk through these streets today is a form of public entertainment as well as a lesson in cultural history.

Only a few decades after it was born, the Annex lost its social cachet and slipped downward; the leading families moved to newer suburbs. Some of the great houses found new uses – the masterpiece that David Roberts designed for the whisky baron George Gooderham at 135 St. George Street became the York

Club. Others, less fortunate, were turned into rooming houses, their interiors chopped into tiny rooms, and some of the best disappeared entirely – the Queen Anne mansion of the philanthropist Sir Edmund Walker on St. George Street was torn down in 1969 to make a parking lot for the University of Toronto's John P. Robarts Research Library. (William Dendy, in his book *Lost Toronto,* called this loss "a classic example of the philistinism that Walker had hoped to eradicate by supporting and encouraging that same university.")

When a new fashion for living downtown took hold in the 1960s, it returned to the Annex much of its old chic. Today, carefully protected from apartment developers by fierce citizens' groups, it's the habitat of choice for an army of television producers, musicians, professors, and writers. In these streets the most memorable characters of Margaret Atwood (whose novels make living in Toronto far more interesting than it would be otherwise) nourish their bitter memories and repressed anger as they enact the rituals of husband-stealing and revenge. In the Annex lives the great writer on urban affairs, Jane Jacobs, one of Toronto's chief human assets.

If the Annex is a kind of Upper Bohemia, then Rosedale (which we can see to the east of the Annex, past Yonge Street) remains Toronto's ideal of traditional affluence. This is where the characters of that great mythologist of the Canadian spirit, Robertson Davies, live their intricately braided lives. Its hundreds of Neo-Georgian and Tudor-Revival houses were built for the newly rich only eighty or ninety years ago, but they now evoke the phrase "old money" – which usually means a fortune made by someone's great-grandfather in meat packing or retailing. Amateur linguists claim that the residents speak their own dialect, a quasi-English honk learned in private school, and amateur geographers claim that no district this side of Tokyo is harder for a stranger to navigate; few Torontonians ever master the Rosedale street plan.

Rosedale long ago ceded its position as the core of rich Toronto (there are much grander houses in newer suburbs) but it remains typical of Toronto in one way: only the people who live there ever understand how it works, and that's the way they like it. In a less obvious way, much of Toronto seems to go out of its way to obscure itself. It can be sly and deceptive, shielding its nature behind barriers of reticence developed during its former life as a colonial outpost. The CN Tower speaks for the self-assertive side of Toronto, but another, more shadowy Toronto lives on. The truth of it can be found through studying the social equivalent of geological strata – it's somewhere between the layers of old and new, natural and human-made, British and post-British.

FROM THE TOWER, familiar downtown landmarks are strikingly transformed. The brightly painted boxes on top of the CBC building reveal their unattractive gray roofs. A clutter of electronic equipment dominates the top of Edward Durrell Stone's sleek First Canadian Place. The towers of the Toronto-Dominion Centre, which address King Street and Wellington Street with dark elegance, look messy from above, the service equipment on the roofs strewn around without thought. The CN Tower shows us a city in apparent disarray, a city that seems to be the haphazard result of a series of accidents.

With a little difficulty we can pick out, in the dense business district, the building from which the city viewed itself two generations ago. At King and Yonge, a fifty-seven-storey tower dominates Commerce Court, an office complex near the centre of financial Toronto. This is a 1970s International Style skyscraper, the work of I. M. Pei, that suave prince of modernism; recently it was redesigned at ground level by Eberhard Zeidler, in an attempt to make it more appealing by softening the severity of Pei's design and eliminating the wind-tunnel effect that often made walking through the square an ordeal. From the street it appears to be one among a dozen or so gleaming towers erected downtown during the greatest growth period in local history, from the 1960s to the late 1980s. A closer look reveals that this cluster also includes what is, by Toronto standards, a skyscraper of great antiquity: the Canadian Bank of Commerce Building, thirty-four storeys tall, in its day the highest building in what was then the British Empire. It was designed in the 1920s by the firm of York & Sawyer, the leader among New York bank architects. Today, renamed Commerce Court North, it's dwarfed by the Pei structure and ignored by many who pass it. Those who stop to examine it may discover that it embodies a moment of exhilarating optimism, when Toronto's dreams were focused on a future that would be both hugely prosperous and supremely dignified.

The old Commerce Court North meets the street with great panache. On a grandly Romanesque arch, stone carvers placed a garland of bees, beehives, squirrels, and other nostalgic reminders of the time when banks believed it their duty to encourage industry and thrift rather than profligate spending. The visitor, having absorbed this florid performance, can enter the immense, barrel-vaulted banking hall. Dressed in roseate stone with gilt mouldings, the room neatly expresses the infinite self-regard of bankers. It was modeled on the Baths of Caracalla in Rome, but today seems more likely to evoke a religious mood; in another era, the impulses that created this space would have been devoted to building cathedrals.

At the top of Commerce Court North, on its observation deck, there's something much stranger and more eccentric, a work of art that has often found its way into historic Toronto photography: four gigantic male heads carved in stone, each of them twenty-four feet high, wearing beards ten feet long. They were designed at the architect's office and executed by Toronto stone carvers on the site. The reason for their size is obvious (they had to be seen from the street, 450 feet below) but their meaning remains obscure. The designer seems to have created these money-gods by combining bits of Easter Island, hints of Aztec, and a touch of Hollywood Indian. They are formidable, and they make a good try at looking wise, but no one knows quite why they are there. Immaculately restored in the 1970s, that building became the second layer of Commerce Court. Alas, the observation deck and its sculpture are now inaccessible. From certain angles we can still glimpse the gods, but the observation deck became a casualty of the towers around it. It closed when nearby buildings grew so tall they ruined the view.

FROM ATOP THE CN TOWER, we can make out only a few traces of Toronto's greatest secret: its topography, the strange chunks of woodland that a visitor suddenly encounters in odd corners of the city. To a superficial observer, Toronto seems flat and overly organized, a bureaucrat's dream of efficient urbanity, but certain experiences hint at another kind of reality embedded beneath the grid plan. If you drive along Rosedale Valley Road, close to the center of town, you pass through a stretch of untended forest; a few seconds later, you find yourself confronting the gleaming towers of Yonge Street. Out for a walk, perhaps in a suburb, you reach the end of a street that should logically lead to another street and instead find yourself looking down into what appears to be wilderness. Or you visit an ordinary-looking house on an ordinary-looking street in the middle of the city and discover that the kitchen opens onto an unruly forest. These fragmentary encounters reveal Toronto's green underside, the hundreds of ravines that constitute the organic and subterranean life of the city, nature beneath culture.

Perhaps this secret underground world is the place where the spirit of Toronto has traditionally been generated. Jan Morris, that remarkable Welsh travel writer, noted some years ago that visitors and immigrants find Toronto's reticence oppressive. She called Toronto "the most undemonstrative city I know, and the least inquisitive," a place of clubs and cliques, "armour-plated against the individual." Old Torontonians can say in their defence that since the 1950s Toronto has absorbed successive waves of immigrants, who have reshaped every aspect of city life. Yet even the oldest of Old Torontonians would probably admit that Morris's accusation contains an element of truth.

What accounts for this reticence? Morris blamed the flatness of the landscape, but Toronto is not flat. Her mistake, though, is understandable. We have so carefully disguised the topography that she, like many visitors, missed it entirely. And this ravine world is paralleled by the tunnel system. Neither can be called coherent, neither can be understood without careful observation. Both are quintessentially Torontonian – as Torontonian, one might say, as the CN Tower.

FROM THE TOWER, as the restaurant revolves back towards the lake, a major surprise reveals itself to those who imagine they know the city: the Leslie Street Spit, the most remarkable topographic change in this century, now called Tommy Thompson Park. A headland reaching five kilometres into Lake Ontario, the spit was created mainly out of sand and clay taken from gigantic holes dug as the new city was being built. Some four million loads of material have been dumped there, and at the height of the building boom in the 1980s it was receiving 400 to 500 truckloads a day. From their perch in the revolving restaurant, visitors can reflect that the very earth excavated to make the CN Tower has now sprung to life in the spit. The spit is downtown Toronto's basement, dumped into the lake. Urban detritus – gigantic chunks of mangled concrete, discarded hydro-electric poles, whatever the city threw aside as it remade itself – now forms the edges that protect the spit from the ravages of winter storms.

A romantic myth has grown up around the Leslie Street Spit, a myth of spontaneity, of a city renewing its southern edge by humbly surrendering to natural forces. And from ground level, at the south end of an old industrial area, it does have the look of an inspired accident, landscaped by the whims of nature. Seeds borne on the wind have grown into a vast tangle of trees, shrubs, and grasses. Armies of raccoons, rabbits, rats, skunks, and mink have occupied it, and even a colony of coyotes has arrived, by God knows what devious route. It's a new urban wilderness, visited by some 290 bird species, at least forty-five of which breed there. Some, in fact, breed all too well. Ring-billed gulls find the spit so accommodating to their needs that they threaten to exclude other birds; the Metropolitan Toronto and Region Conservation Authority has had to fight them off with (as the authority puts it) "falconry, pyrotechnical devices and mock gulls," techniques that have so far limited the gull colonies to a tolerable size.

From the ground the spit appears to jut carelessly southward into the lake. But a glance from the CN Tower reveals, first, that it reaches westward, almost parallel to the city, eventually stretching in front of the southern beach of Ward's Island, creating a kind of lagoon where there was open water only twenty years ago. From the tower the spit also turns out to be more deliberate than legend suggests. It's a carefully sculptured series of bays and inlets, with 100 boat moorings on its scalloped edges. It looks, in fact, like the basis for an elaborate property development scheme of the twenty-first or twenty-second century.

This wilderness is spontaneous in only one sense: like so many major features of Toronto, it is not what it set out to be. In 1959, optimistic local opinion held that the recently built St. Lawrence Seaway would bring a rush of prosperity to the Port of Toronto. Accordingly, the coastal engineers of the Toronto Harbour Commission laid out the beginnings of the spit as an extension of the outer harbour. But port traffic never reached the expected level, and the spit was unnecessary. By the time this was understood it was already a fair-sized headland, and in 1973 – having no other purpose – it became recreational land. After that it seemed natural to let it continue growing. And so it does.

MODERN TORONTO is an accidental city in many other ways. It's a place where major events happen by inadvertence and momentous decisions are made in ignorance of their consequences. The CN Tower itself is just such a surprise – and yet a surprise typical of Toronto. It began as the glorious centrepiece of a vast development that never happened. It turned out to be (just like the spit) something its original planners did not envisage. And its ostensible purpose – distributing television signals – became almost irrelevant not long after it was completed.

It also remains largely anonymous. Most people know something about Gustave Eiffel, the engineer who left his name on the most famous landmark produced by nineteenth-century Europe, but the millions of people who glance at the CN Tower every day apparently never wonder who built it. It is as if nature placed it there. To this day it remains possible to write a lyrical newspaper article extolling "the serene elegance of its silhouette" and its "forbidding modern majesty" (John Bentley Mays, *The Globe and Mail,* September 24, 1994) without naming the architect whose design is being praised.

Many engineers and executives were involved in planning the CN Tower, but the designer is Ned Baldwin, now part of the firm of Baldwin & Franklin. An American-born architect, he began practicing in Toronto in the 1960s as a partner with John Andrews. The Andrews firm was assigned, along with the Webb Zerafa Menkes Housden Partnership, to plan the development that would surround the CN Tower.

That project was one of the titanic might-have-beens of urban development. It was conceived in the 1960s, when the centre of gravity in downtown Toronto was about to shift westward. The shift led eventually to (in rough chronological order) the Metro Toronto Convention Centre, Roy Thomson Hall, the SkyDome, the CBC Broadcasting Centre, Metro Hall, and the Princess of Wales Theatre. But in the late 1960s a more controlled and much more ambitious development was imagined. The idea was to build, on about 190 acres of what planners traditionally call the Railway Lands, a collection of commercial and residential buildings that would reunite the city with the lake. Sections of it were briefly known as Southtown and CityPlace. There were plans to incorporate other land, owned by local government, the Toronto Harbour Commission, and the federal government. For this purpose, Canadian National (CN) and Canadian Pacific Limited (CP) set up a joint venture company, Metro Centre.

The idea was born in the Toronto planning department in the 1950s. Then as now, railroad tracks and vast railroad yards stood in the way of Toronto's natural development, cutting short at Front Street the southward movement of the city. The Toronto planners approached the railroads to ask whether the vast wasteland of tracks, or at least a good part of it, could be moved outside the city core. The railroads said no, they were essential. The city then began working on a plan to go over the tracks by developing a giant deck that would rise up around Front Street, holding walkways and new buildings, providing a kind of doorway to the lake. It would be done with the help of the Harbour Commission and Canadian Steamship Lines, using waterfront land that CSL controlled. In the mid-1960s the city and some of the property owners commissioned a plan from John B. Parkin Associates, a gigantic A-frame arching over the railway lands.

At that point the railways decided to produce their own plan. Having reconsidered, they now discovered they could move most of their yards to the suburbs. They had seen what profit could be devised from railroad lands in New York and around Place Ville Marie in Montreal. They commissioned a plan of truly astonishing size. They would move the railroad corridor to the south, tear down the old Union Station, build office towers near Yonge Street and apartment towers near Bathurst Street. All this was presented to the city and the public as Metro Centre, the name later attached to the development that contains the Metro government headquarters.

At the core of the plan was a deal. The city would allow higher and denser development than the official plan called for, and in return the railroads would do something remarkable: they would become invisible. Some tracks would be moved and others would be buried in tunnels, at great expense. For the first time since the 1850s, railroad tracks would cease to be a major element in downtown Toronto. Metro Centre would be the largest building project in the history of Canada. If it failed – if for instance, the design proved monotonous and unappealing – the failure would be colossal. Nevertheless, city council liked it, and in 1970 decided to enter a partnership with the railroads. The idea gathered momentum. In the eyes of many people involved, it seemed to be the inevitable next step in the remaking of Toronto.

It was stopped by the 1972 election, which brought a new kind of city council. The reform movement that had been born a few years earlier, after William Dennison defeated Philip Givens in the 1966 election for mayor, now came to power; one reformer, David Crombie, became mayor. Alderman John Sewell had been arguing against Metro Centre for years, and now he began attracting support for his view that it was much too good a deal for the developers. In his 1972 book, *Up Against City Hall,* Sewell wrote, "The city fathers were giving large chunks of land to the railways for a pittance," in "the greatest swindle we can expect in Toronto in our life-time." Aside from city property, Metro Centre would occupy land owned by the Toronto Harbour Commission and CN, both public agencies. As for Canadian Pacific, a private corporation, it probably had more land than it deserved, having received it in nineteenth-century grants for dubious reasons. Should all of this property be used for commercial gain? And then there was the question of Union Station. Toronto was just beginning to learn that historic buildings were worth preserving. Union Station was a great monument, a splendid example of its type, and shouldn't be carelessly thrown aside.

The climate for large-scale development of these lands suddenly grew cool. The city began dragging its feet. Finally, in 1975, Metro Centre was abandoned. But not the tower. It was to have been the focal point of Metro Centre, and in a moment of enthusiasm the railroads had gone ahead with it, perhaps to make a public show of their confidence that something magnificent was about to happen here. It was a bold move that failed. By the time everyone understood the failure, the CN Tower was reaching into the clouds.

THE IDEA of a tower had begun with the Canadian Broadcasting Corporation. In the late 1960s the CBC television tower, next to the old radio building on Jarvis Street in 1952, was no longer capable of sending a clear signal to the growing Toronto region. After considering a site north of the city, the broadcast engineers decided that the ideal location was downtown. The CBC approached CN, proposing a partnership in the building of a new structure (the CBC later withdrew). Norman J. MacMillan, chairman and president of Canadian National, liked the idea of a tower that would serve broadcasters and make a commanding signature for Metro Centre. MacMillan personally made the decision to build the tower – made it without knowing where the revenues would come from, what would be built around it, or what role the tower would play in the life of the city.

Nor did he understand the cost. The first budget was $21 million. By the time ground was broken it had reached $29 million. The final cost was $59 million. By then, however, those figures were not as alarming as they might appear. Something else had happened: revenue projections were growing even faster than construction costs. The managers planning the project had discovered, to their surprise, that they were not building a communications tower, or even the logo of a property development. A structure that began life as an adjunct to the broadcasting business had acquired independent drawing power. In the beginning, as Baldwin says, "We were naive in not knowing what a major symbol we were building." As the tower went up it attracted the kind of attention that could be translated into a form of mass entertainment. Long before it opened, the planners realized they were building a tourist attraction, a vertical theme park.

The television and radio business turned out to be incidental. The tower still sends television signals through the air, but most people in Toronto never see them; cable subscribers get pictures pulled down from satellites onto the roof of First Canadian Place and then distributed by land lines. Even in the early years, broadcasting (including the signals of FM radio) provided only 15 per cent of the tower's revenue; now the percentage is down to 12 per cent. Today the tower management could make more money by evicting the broadcasters and devoting the space they use to new attractions – a heretical notion that occasionally makes furtive appearances in corporate planning discussions.

Early marketing reports suggesting that the real money was in tourism proved correct. Before the opening, the owners were counting on about a million visitors a year, but the actual number has always been higher than that; the average now is 1.7 million. Long before the last pieces were in place, Baldwin and his colleagues were visiting Walt Disney World to study tourist management and crowd control. Even so, they made mistakes. Given the chance to do it again, Baldwin would put another floor in the pod, for private functions; today the tower turns down a lot of business it could accommodate if it had more space. And he would provide an even better view from the restaurant by replacing its exterior columns with a cantilevered design.

At the start, Baldwin and his colleagues had little guidance. MacMillan told them only that he wanted a revolving restaurant and observation decks, inside and out, as well as the space for broadcasting equipment. Otherwise, they were on their own. They emphasized streamlining, to minimize wind resistance, and on the main concrete pillar they put fins that produce an elegant flaring effect. "I was conscious," Baldwin remembers, "that I was inflicting this structure on everybody's view. My preoccupation was to make sure it was good looking from a distance."

The tower paid off the construction debt in fifteen years, a notable accomplishment, and then began pouring millions into the CN treasury – $5 million in 1994. To this moment it remains one of the busiest places in the city, a success that surely illustrates the triumph of symbolic power over circumstances. It remains badly located, set down in a physical environment that's all wrong for a tourist attraction. An early press release, published when Metro Centre was still a lively possibility, said the tower "will be set in parkland, with landscaped terraces sloping to a large reflecting pool." It was to have been the focus of a grand esplanade, but nothing like that happened. The tower became an orphan, isolated in a hostile environment; the main rail corridor, which was supposed to go far to the south, remained just to the north of the tower's base. During construction, as Ned Baldwin has said, "We realized that we were building a tourist attraction in the middle of a railway yard – and it was impossible to get to it." Metro Centre would have extended John Street south to meet The Esplanade, but now John Street was not coming south and The Esplanade was not being developed. As Baldwin wrote in a 1976 article for *Canadian Architect,* "Under such ludicrous circumstances Canadian National would hardly have chosen this location to build." Baldwin put a pedestrian bridge across the railway tracks so that people could reach the entrance from Front Street, but the surroundings felt constricted. They still do.

And yet, the tower has not had an unprofitable year since it opened. Attendance and profits fell in the late 1980s and early 1990s, showing the combined effects of the recession and increasingly fierce competition for entertainment spending; the SkyDome moved in next door and ate up a lot of the tower's parking. Inside, the tower acquired a shabby, worn look, and sometimes visiting it was an ordeal. On the busiest days of the busiest season – say, a Saturday in early August – people lined up for four or five hours to get to the observation deck. A marketing survey reported that they thought it worth visiting once but not again.

In 1992 the CN installed new management, dedicated to making the tower "Toronto's premiere family entertainment destination." John Tevlin, the new president, cleaned it up and painted it, put in a new food court, renovated the observation deck, developed a ticketing system that cut the line-ups, and, most recently, redesigned the revolving restaurant. Attendance soon began rising again. But the reception space at ground level – complete with video arcade, souvenir shop, and The MindWarp Theatre – still feels heavy-handed, a too obvious system for extracting every last dollar from every last tourist's pocket. Much of the tiny outdoor space next to the tower was turned over, by some unfathomable executive decision, to miniature golf. Nevertheless, the tower continues to bring tourists. About a quarter of them are from elsewhere in Canada, a quarter each from the U.S. and Europe, 15 per cent from Toronto, and the rest from as far away as Sydney and Tokyo; in recent years Asian tourists have been growing more numerous.

A few visitors turn out to be emissaries from distant countries who imagine that they should have something like the CN Tower back home, perhaps on an even grander scale. Over the years Baldwin has designed towers for Singapore and Kuwait, Jakarta and Las Vegas. One of them, for Kokura in west Japan, would go up 750 metres, half again as high as the CN Tower. None has actually been built except the Vegas World Stratosphere Tower, which (as of this writing) remains unfinished. The Chinese have lately talked about building a rough copy of the CN Tower. In countries without cable-TV, a communications tower still makes sense, but the increasing possibility of direct-to-home satellite television inhibits some would-be builders.

- Despite scores of feasibility studies in many countries, the CN Tower remains unique. The daring, optimism, foolhardiness, and dumb luck that made it possible haven't come together a second time, anywhere in the world. Perhaps it could have happened only in Toronto.

3

The Hidden City

IN THE DARK early morning of Saturday, October 16, 1954, the worst natural disaster in the history of Toronto reached Raymore Drive. Hurricane Hazel, born near Grenada eleven days earlier, had poured eighteen centimetres of water on the city. On Friday night people living downtown thought it was no more than a heavy storm, but in the raw new suburbs the rain soon began to feel more like a biblical flood. Streets and backyards turned to mud, parking lots became lagoons, and every creek spilled over its banks. In many places, chunks of floating debris came together and clogged a river or stream, creating a temporary dam. The water would pause for a while, build up strength, then suddenly burst through as a violent floodcrest. The deadliest of the floodcrests hit Raymore Drive, a street in Etobicoke where houses were placed, with tragic foolishness, on the floodplain beside the Humber River. A wave more than six metres high swept away sixteen brick houses, killing thirty-six people. Across the Toronto region another forty-seven died in similar ways.

The low-lying and dangerous section of Raymore Drive has since become Raymore Park, one of a long chain of parks on the Humber – a change that neatly symbolizes the hurricane's long-term effect. This accident of nature was a turning point, the most influential one-day event in the planning history of modern Toronto. It forced the city to acknowledge and deal with the central fact of local topography – the network of wooded, steep-sloped ravines that were carved out of the sand and clay on which Toronto sits by streams that flowed south from the Oak Ridges moraine after the last Ice Age. The hurricane demonstrated not only that the streams needed to be respected but that the ravines were a distinct element in the cityscape, requiring special attention.

In pre-Hazel days, Toronto built houses in the ravines, ran roads through them, installed factories and brickworks in them, used them as garbage dumps, and put apartment buildings on their slopes. A 1960 study published by the city planning board noted that, since the founding of Toronto, 840 of the 1,900 acres of original ravine lands had been eaten up by houses, factories and roads. By the time those figures appeared, the place of the ravines in the imagination of the city was already changing. Hurricane Hazel led to the creation of the Metropolitan Toronto and Region Conservation Authority, which has ever since been buying up ravine properties and turning them into parks and conservation lands. By alerting both politicians and public, the hurricane rescued thousands of acres around the ravines from the realm of private property and made them public land. That process eventually became a significant part of Toronto's transformation into a city conscious of its public spaces. Toronto's park system today is much more extensive than it would be if the storm had passed over the city on that night in 1954. As Helen Juhola of the Toronto Field Naturalists' Club has said of Hurricane Hazel: "It's wonderful what it gave us."

The landscape architect Michael Hough wrote of the ravines in *Out of Place: Restoring Identity to the Regional Landscape,* "They have become Toronto's stamp of individuality." They make Toronto a major flyover place for birds and provide spaces of cool and quiet in many corners of the city. They are also the breeding places and retreats of a vast army of raccoons, the city's largest wild animal population. More important, they give a sense of place to Toronto and to many of its neighbourhoods. "One reason I think Toronto is a marvelous place," Hough has said, "is that it has this wonderful sense of identity." The identity comes largely from the experience of using ravines over many years and from the sharp contrast between life on the streets and life a few steps away in the ravines. "You are on the flat," as Hough says, "and then you drop down, and everything vanishes." There's nothing quite like them anywhere else. No other big city has so much nature woven with such intricate thoroughness through its urban fabric.

The ravines are to Toronto what canals are to Venice and hills are to San Francisco. They are the heart of the city's emotional geography, and understanding Toronto requires an understanding of the ravines. In the republic of childhood they represent a savage foreign state, a place of adventure and terror. A ravine provides a Torontonian's first glimpse of something resembling wilderness; often it is also the earliest intimation of nearby danger. A Toronto child usually learns about the ravines from an anxious parent's warning that evil strangers lurk down there. They can indeed be places of danger, but the act of entering a ravine, often in defiance of parental orders, has for many Torontonians been an essential part of growing up.

I remember it well. The thrill of disobedience fades quickly, replaced by the eerie sensation of landing in a distinct world, close to the streets but radically different. You slide down leaf-clad slopes, feel squishy earth beneath your feet, and arrive at the bottom in sunlight filtered by thick stands of trees. The sounds of traffic become a murmur in the background and then disappear. A stream flows through the silence, emerging from nowhere and then vanishing mysteriously into a pipe.

As unruly as a child's mind, the ravine becomes the ideal site for Toronto dreams. Asphalt and cement are real to city children, but wildflowers, ferns, and chipmunks evoke exotic fantasies. Glen Stewart Ravine, south of Kingston Road in the Beach district, nourished my own imagination. In my ten-year-old eyes, the forest on those slopes went on forever, though I can now walk through it in ten minutes. The Toronto parks department has tamed it by providing nature trails, a wooden staircase where once I slid in mud and snow, even a brochure that tells visitors not to stray from the paths. My old ravine needs this kind of protection (kids sliding down hills are hell on bushes), and it amply rewards those who go there to look for the yellow-bellied sapsucker or the spotted touch-me-not. If it now offers charm and enlightenment in place of the wildness I found there in the 1940s, it's probably a fair exchange.

After Torontonians grow up, and even after they learn that there are grander forests in the world, the ravines retain their mystery. No one ever completely explores the hundreds of ravines whose streams feed the six rivers of Metropolitan Toronto (from Etobicoke Creek on the west edge to the Rouge River on the east); in fact, no one has counted them. Acquiring a detailed knowledge of them would be the work of a lifetime.

Because of the ravines, a Torontonian can explore nature with an ease that's impossible for many people living in the country. Outside the boundaries of Metropolitan Toronto you can rarely follow a river valley for any distance without running into private-property signs. Thanks to Hurricane Hazel, you can now walk the banks of the Humber River all the way from Bloor Street to Highway 401 – though only after you learn how to do it, and find your way around the obstacles that have been placed in your path. You can also walk the Don River for most of a day. If you start from the lake and then turn west at the forks of the Don you can go past the Ontario Science Centre and through Sunnybrook Park all the way to the doors of Glendon College in the suburbs.

Along the way you may discover that the ravine lands are still evolving, in response to human pressures. In many cases, natural growth overcomes human intrusion. The city channels a storm sewer through a pipe and then lets nature hide the evidence – and nature, given enough time, obliges. Since farming ended on the upper Don a few decades ago, the environment has been slowly returning to something like the wilderness it once was.

Almost anywhere in the ravines, vegetation shows the effects of human contact. Roadsalt, for instance, works striking changes. Sluicing down the storm sewers into the river valleys, it kills many plants, leaving space for others. As a result, wild plants that were mainly unknown in southern Ontario a couple of generations ago now grow profusely in the ravines. The scarlet pimpernel, *Anagallis arvensis,* shows up in the Don Valley and under bridges elsewhere, having presumably traveled from its former coastal homes on anything from the feet of birds to the undercarriages of trucks. It flourishes now because more effete competitors have been eliminated by roadsalt.

FOUR DECADES AFTER Hurricane Hazel, we still occasionally nibble away at the ravines, though in less spectacular ways. Joey Slinger of the Toronto *Star,* an eloquent writer on Toronto and its ravines, has proclaimed the First Rule of Toronto Conservation: "All the ravines are threatened all the time." People often buy what the real-estate ads call "a handsome ravine lot" and then scar the landscape by leveling their property for a swimming pool or a tennis court, leaving their neighbours to wonder why they wanted a ravine lot in the first place. Even governments sometimes use the ravines carelessly. The City of Toronto officially frowns on any construction on the banks of rivers or the sides of ravines, but in the early 1990s the parks department built an extension of Riverdale Farm on the slope of the Don. Ironically, its purpose was public instruction on the interpretation of nature.

That sort of mistake would happen less frequently if Toronto understood the natural riches of the valleys and ravines. We remain unnecessarily ignorant because people are not made welcome in many of them. Too often, there's no obvious point of entry: the system resembles a private club that you can use only if you know someone who will escort you in. If you happen to find yourself at the busy corner of Broadview and Danforth Avenues, for instance, you may realize that you're looking down at not only a flat playground but an interesting river valley. You're close to it, but how do you penetrate it? Only with difficulty. To go north on the Don you can first walk for fifteen boring minutes up Broadview to Mortimer Avenue, and enter there. To go south you must get down to the playing field, cross it, cross a footbridge, then make your way into the system. No visible information is provided at Broadview and Danforth about either of these routes.

Bad as it is, though, that's one of the best points to get close to the Don. In some places, you can't reach it at all – there's not one entry point between the Martin Goodman Trail at the bottom of the city and Riverdale Park. It's as if we wanted to hide the river and forget it. As Michael Hough has pointed out, Toronto has an unfortunate tradition of concealing the reasons that it was originally settled. The Don, which helped make this part of the world habitable, is the obvious example. For a long time it was a river to admire and celebrate, and in the 1870s Torontonians sang "Come to the Vale of the Beautiful Don," a ballad written by an elegant Englishwoman, Mrs. G. A. Gilbert –

Oh! come to woodlands 'neath their shades deep and free,
Where sings the lone wild-bird in the green linden tree.
Come! linger thy footfall where the waters flow on,
By the banks and the glens of the beautiful Don!

IT'S BEEN a long time since anyone expressed such sentiments about the Don. Late in the nineteenth century the city straightened it, forcing the water into a narrow channel so that the land next to it could be used by the railway. That was the beginning of the valley's downfall, and the city has been trying to ignore its most important river ever since. In this century pollution made it "the Dirty Don," a listless brown stream. By the 1920s Toronto had turned away in shame: buildings put up on the river didn't even have windows looking out on it. In 1991 a task-force report published by the city, *Bringing Back the Don,* described the results of a public-opinion survey: "'Polluted' was the most frequently used word to describe the river and the valley. Other negative terms and expressions used included 'smelly,' 'dirty' and 'dangerous' (some talked of dead bodies, suicides and the possibility of children being molested). Some participants described the river and the valley as a receptacle for rubbish.... Some were bemused by the number of shopping carts they see down there."

Regeneration, the 1992 report of David Crombie's royal commission on the waterfront, described the condition of the valley of the Lower Don: "Chain-link fences line the shores of the river, and log booms at its mouth contain the flotsam that surges down the river during rainstorms. Water and sediment quality in the river is poor, as is wildlife habitat. Access to the shores is limited and uninviting, and only a few hardy souls walk or cycle along it." In Michael Hough's view the Don will be reclaimed as a self-respecting river only after we make it visible and accessible. *Bringing Back the Don* suggested that we begin reviving the river by constructing steps down to it beside every bridge. Today the problem of the Don is psychological as well as environmental. It needs to be re-installed in the image of the city that Torontonians carry in their minds. The Don, like all the ravines and river valleys, will survive only if the citizens appreciate it.

THE RAVINES APPEAR, from time to time, in the work of fiction writers looking for a place where characters can escape the rigidities of Toronto life. In *Minus Time*, Catherine Bush's 1993 novel, a young man describes his rebellious adolescence in the suburbs: "When I was thirteen, I ran away from home and lived in the ravines by myself for over a week." He remembers causing a public stir. "I was called the Ravine Boy in the news, I had my picture in the paper, and afterward the police were kind of freaked out that they hadn't been able to find me. I started out in Wilket Creek Park and made my way down, south of the Science Centre. Down toward the Don Valley Parkway...after a week I got bored and lonely, and I figured my parents had a chance to really miss me and even think I was dead, so I made my way to a supermarket parking lot and convinced a woman to drive me home."

An essay by Hugh Hood, in *The Governor's Bridge is Closed*, depicts the Toronto ravines as a topographical equivalent of the human unconscious. Psychology uses the metaphor of a labyrinth to describe hidden caves of the mind, but: "In Toronto there are real labyrinths (make psychology of them if you please) which uncoil and connect all the way across town." In *Toronto Places: A Context for Urban Design*, the architect Larry Richards describes the ravines as "a secret Toronto embedded in its geography – what has been referred to as 'San Francisco upside down'... carved through the land are twenty-nine deep ravines and valleys – San Francisco's hills in reverse. These powerful, winding cuts are well known to Toronto residents: but to the casual visitor they are almost invisible."

Why are they invisible? Two centuries ago, Governor John Graves Simcoe imposed a military-style street grid on the new town of York, around Parliament and Front Streets. That made sense, because the land near the water's edge was flat. But later the city extended the grid plan indefinitely (except, notably, in Rosedale), ignoring the river valleys and ravines or obliterating them with highways and landfill. A more imaginative city plan would have used the local topography as an organizing principle, building the districts around the valleys and waterways; that would have led naturally to a more intelligent use of Lake Ontario, the eventual destination of all the waterways.

Instead, Toronto on its worst days has had the effrontery to regard its rivers and ravines as an inconvenience, an unfortunate barrier in the way of progress. We have managed to make Toronto appear topographically uneventful, except for the escarpment that runs along Davenport Road below Casa Loma (the mock-medieval castle built in 1914) and eventually turns into the Scarborough Bluffs. It is as if Toronto were ashamed of the shape that nature provided.

Torontonians have difficulty seeing their environment. We look at it in pieces and fail, through inattention, to see it whole. We rarely think of Toronto as a forest city, but the forest continues to wind through our districts. Toronto, in fact, is the setting of a kind of arboreal drama: the southern Carolinian forest, having made its way around the western end of Lake Ontario, meets the eastern mixed forest of the St. Lawrence River Valley somewhere around High Park. To the sharp-eyed and the curious, this fact and many others reveal themselves in the infinite variety of the ravines. And one day, perhaps, the presence of the ravines will force Torontonians to redraw their mental picture of the place where they live. Eventually we may decide that Toronto, properly understood, is not a big city that contains some parks but a big park that contains a city.

THE LABYRINTH BENEATH downtown Toronto is in its way as complicated as the ravines, and presents an equally deceptive face. Enter it almost anywhere and it looks simple to the point of banality, a chunk of suburban shopping centre placed below grade. And the underground city is simple, for many of the 100,000 or so people who work in the buildings upstairs and routinely walk through the tunnels. But for a tourist, or a Torontonian who has never used it before, or even for regular users who happen to stray from their normal paths, the system is as disorienting as the Vienna sewers where Orson Welles hid in *The Third Man*. This network of malls – some 1,100 stores and services, spread along ten kilometres of make-believe streets – has become the urban equivalent of a trackless wasteland. Like the ravines, the underground serves those who have learned its secret ways. And like the ravines, it remains largely inaccessible to those who haven't.

It has been growing haphazardly since the early 1970s, and with each year has become both a larger success and a larger embarrassment. Those involved in building it may see it as a triumph because they know how much ingenious planning went into moving the underground wires and gas pipes. But it remains a bewildering maze. One result is that it's less used than it might be – empty in the evenings, lonely on Saturday, lonelier on Sunday, a potential tourist attraction that attracts few tourists. As town planning, it seems to offer proof of inadequate leadership. The dozens of developers and architects who built it created tunnels of many colours, heights and widths, and it seldom occurred to them that they should erect signs explaining where any given tunnel led. The result is a glaring case of municipal inadvertence.

And yet it's also a monument to a town planner's vision. In the 1960s, when it was a vague proposal, no one imagined that the tunnels would ever stretch as far as they now do, over to Metro Centre in the west. But one planner, Matthew Lawson, imagined that much of the future of downtown was below grade. He was city planning commissioner from 1954 to 1967, when Toronto began rebuilding its business centre. As Lawson saw it, the growth that was coming presented several problems. The sidewalks were too crowded – by 1960, people were spilling into the gutters at rush hour – and there was no affordable way to widen them. Dry cleaners, restaurants, and other services were vanishing from the streets because they didn't fit into the new corporate aesthetic. Those who were putting up buildings, especially banks, didn't want the logos of hamburger joints and camera shops cluttering their elegant facades and blurring their corporate identities. Yet a business district without the variety provided by stores and restaurants can be cold and forbidding as well as inconvenient. Toronto already knew that, thanks to University Avenue, a sterile planning disaster from the 1920s and 1930s.

Enemies of Lawson's achievement can say that he, too, ignored human needs. He put the people underground, in rabbit warrens without natural light. Why did he not put the cars in tunnels and give the streets to human beings? He certainly considered the idea. A report published by his office suggested that Toronto could turn the downtown core into a huge pedestrian precinct and place the roads below grade. Planning textbooks favoured that solution, but it's never been applied on a large scale. Lawson realized that burying the roads would involve a period of painful disruption and require a colossal financial commitment that he couldn't imagine the city and the province making. He also took a skeptical view of the textbook solutions. "Planners like to see people on the street because it looks nice," he remarked in 1992, discussing the development of his idea. "They're not thinking of what the people want and need to do." People want to be able to get easily from place to place, and they want to be able to buy computer paper or egg rolls without fuss. They also want to avoid bad weather when they can. In Lawson's view, the underground works for those who use it regularly. "The concourse system knits downtown together – when you are in one of those buildings you are, in a sense, in all of them." He doesn't think the lack of natural light is a problem. The system has several concourse spaces reached by ample natural light, but these don't seem to be any more popular than spaces lit entirely by electricity.

In the late 1950s Lawson began describing the virtues of below-grade concourses and the possibility of underground links. He was encouraged by Place Ville Marie in Montreal, I. M. Pei's sleek, prosperous combination of below-grade shopping and expensive office space, built on seven acres of former CNR land. Pierre Berton wrote in The Toronto *Star* in 1962 that Place Ville Marie had put Montreal a decade ahead of Toronto in downtown planning. That year I wrote a *Maclean's* magazine cover story suggesting that it represented the wave of the future. This publicity helped Lawson persuade developers to include underground malls in their buildings, and to think about the day when they might all be connected. He convinced the planners of the Toronto-Dominion Centre that underground shopping would work, and when the Richmond-Adelaide Centre was being planned he promised its developers that if an underground path were eventually created, he would try to point it towards their concourse. The city assembled the land opposite the New City Hall for development (it eventually became the Sheraton Centre) and specified that the developers had to pay for underground walkways north to the City Hall parking garage and south to the Richmond-Adelaide Centre. Elsewhere, at Lawson's suggestion, the city paid half the cost of the tunnels beneath the streets, the other half being shared by owners of the buildings being joined.

Lawson's plans were well laid by the time he left the city in 1967 to become a private consultant, and many of them came to fruition in the 1970s. By then, however, the underground city had acquired some powerful enemies, notably the reformers on city council. They didn't like underground shopping or the cold, blank, windswept plazas being built on the surface. Since they believed the underground was killing street life, they withdrew the 50 per cent subsidy for the tunnels. Later the city provided only a fifth of the cost of one tunnel and nothing for most of the others. But by then the system was beyond halting. The owners of each new building wanted to be connected, whether they had the city's blessing or not. Tenants had come to expect it.

Lawson imagined that the underground city would explain itself to the casual visitor and make clear its relationship to surface streets. For instance, two paths running roughly parallel to King Street might be called South King Alley and North King Alley. Nothing like that happened. It was as if the city were ashamed of the tunnels and wanted them to remain secret. By the 1980s it became clear they badly needed co-ordination.

Consider the story told by a woman who commutes from Oakville on the GO train. She had often read about the marvelously convenient pathways beneath the city, and during the Toronto Transit Commission (TTC) strike of September, 1991, she decided to walk underground from Union Station to the Atrium on Bay at Dundas, the northern border of the system. She couldn't figure out how to do it. As she walked north she kept running into places where the path appeared to end. There were no signs to tell her whether she was under King or Richmond, no signs saying which way was north, and no indication of how to get from one mall to another. It was as if the builders had conspired to keep her from finding the way.

In fact, that was more or less the case. Each building owner wanted her to spend her time and money where she was rather than walk to another owner's property. When she reached First Canadian Place (stretching between King and Adelaide), she found nothing to inform her that to go north she had to stop at the centre of the marble shopping plaza, walk west for a bit, then make a right turn to get into the only tunnel leading north. She assumed, reasonably enough, that the passages would roughly duplicate the streets of the city. They don't. The underground grew haphazardly, following the needs of the real estate market, ignoring the street plan above, so that in the below-grade world the historic grid of Toronto simply dissolves. In the end, she never did find the way. She went back up to the street and walked through the rain.

ONE CITIZEN who has always worried about this problem is the designer Paul Arthur, who was responsible for the influential signage at Expo 67 in Montreal and has ever since been involved in developing the craft that designers call wayfinding. In the early 1980s, Arthur began giving lectures on the chaos of the underground, and in 1985 the city commissioned him to write a report on how it could be made easier to use. In his introduction he wrote that the system was such a crucial part of the city that "no one thinks it can continue much longer as an impenetrable maze." Actually, it continued a good deal longer, the maze growing worse with each extension.

Arthur's report led to a sign program, which was designed by Stuart Ash and Keith Muller and coordinated for the city planning department by Don Sinclair, who did something similar for Calgary's overhead walkways in the 1980s. Putting the system together was a major diplomatic project, since thirty or so corporations, the parking authority, the transit system, and the city had to agree on a series of aesthetic decisions. Along the way there were serious disappointments.

The one thing all citizens would want, and any government would eagerly provide if it could, is a clearly marked way of going directly from, say, Union Station to the Eaton Centre. But the Toronto underground can't have anything like that, because of its peculiar public-but-private nature. While we sometimes speak of "underground streets," most of them are private property, patrolled by private cops, regulated by private rules. You can't picket there, or promote religious causes, or beg, or sleep, as you can in real streets upstairs.

Obviously, the plazas at the concourse levels of commercial buildings are private, but what about the tunnels connecting them? The question isn't academic: in recent winters a few homeless people discovered that the tunnels between buildings are, in some sense, public. They tried to use them for begging and even sleeping, to the consternation of the building owners. Security guards sent them away, but the possibility of a legal issue lingered. The owners had made agreements with the city allowing public access to the tunnels. Did that mean access only for people walking through, or access of the kind we take for granted on the streets? The courts may eventually decide, but the question lurks in the background of negotiations between the city and the landlords. Owners maintain rights by exercising them, and they may decide that too much cooperation with the city will endanger their independence.

Certainly the owners never considered allowing Stuart Ash to put in a series of signs directing the public from the southern to the northern end of the system, the underground equivalent of a highway. That would cause one path to be used more than any other, making its stores rentable at higher rates; some buildings wouldn't get on the highway at all. The owners wanted clarity, but not too much of it.

They managed to obscure even the nature of the project itself, by giving it a meaningless name. Even though everyone has used "underground" in describing it for more than a decade, the owners decided they didn't like the sound of that word. There was something nasty about it, maybe a suggestion of wartime, or sewers, or hippie newspapers. Finally, this subterranean world was given an official name: "PATH: Toronto's Downtown Walkway." That told strangers two or three facts about it, but omitted the most crucial one – that it's below the surface.

IN THE WINTER of 1993-94, nine years or so after it was first outlined, the PATH system was finally installed. It was not a success. One tiny piece of it illustrated what was wrong: a little pylon sign spelling out PATH, in red, orange, blue, and yellow letters, placed outside the Scotia Plaza, on Adelaide Street. It offered no more information, not even an arrow pointing to whatever it signified. The uninitiated would have no way of knowing what it meant. Anyone who guessed that it was trying to say something about the building behind it, and entered the lobby to learn more, could then discover a much smaller PATH sign at the top of an escalator in the lobby. If the visitor's curiosity remained lively enough to sustain a trip to the concourse level below, underground Toronto would begin, reluctantly, to reveal itself.

Before that one little sign could provide help, a visitor needed to know that there was something called PATH, that it could lead through the underground, and that this piece of street furniture was part of it. Enigmatic and easily overlooked, the pylon on Adelaide Street symbolized the persistent difficulty of making the city core easy to use. PATH will change over the years, as the planning department isolates its weak spots, but the bulk of it is now in place. It has turned out to be a largely unsuccessful attempt to create a little pool of clarity in a swamp of conflicting images and signals.

The individual components of PATH – wall signs, wall maps, compasses on the ceilings, outdoor pylons, paper maps that are handed out in the thousands by office buildings and hotels – are well designed and no doubt deserved the merit award they won from the Society for Environmental Graphic Design in the U.S. But taken together they add up to no more than a tentative first step toward coherence. As a system of communications, PATH fails to speak loudly and clearly. It mutters. It's too reticent to do the job, and its inadequacy illustrates the problems involved in imposing a public presence on private property. The civic impulse and the commercial impulse are in competition, and the civic impulse finishes a bad second.

Because of the separate needs of the various landlords, PATH's signs turned out to be too small and too few, and in many cases hard to find even for those looking for them. They are over-shadowed almost everywhere by commercial logos, which are usually four or five times the size of the PATH signs and are often illuminated. The PATH signs are never back-lit, which makes them look less important than the signs that advertise stores. As Ash says, "They're as big as we can make them. Each sign involves much negotiation. Big illuminated signs might be a good idea, but the building owners wouldn't allow them." In the future the city may add more and possibly bigger signs, but so far PATH is a footnote to its surroundings rather than a chapter heading. It fares worst in the Toronto-Dominion Centre, which refuses to allow anything to clash with its own uniform sign identity. For the T-D, Ash redesigned the PATH signs with black backgrounds, making them nearly invisible. In the Eaton Centre, where the visual competition is more intense, he increased the size of his signs. Even there, however, PATH looks like an afterthought.

What the signs say, or don't say, is as important as their design. In most cases they tell you the name of the buildings next to the one you're in; if you are in First Canadian Place, and you find the PATH signs, you'll be told how to get to the T-D Centre or the Toronto Stock Exchange. The trick of using the underground, however, is knowing how to make more distant connections – how to get from, say, Commerce Court to the Eaton Centre. To do that you must head west to the T-D Centre, north to First Canadian Place, then west again before turning north to the Sheraton Centre. There you turn east to the Hudson's Bay Centre, which leads to the Eaton Centre.

The only way to move any distance underground, short of hiring a Sherpa, is to consult the map first and note the three or four buildings on the way to the one you want to reach and the order in which you must pass through them. Without map in hand, PATH remains useless for any but short trips. After hundreds of meetings between planners and building owners, the tunnels remain far more than confusing than they need to be. Even as it tries to make itself more public, underground Toronto remains in many ways a hidden city.

4

Fred Gardiner's Specialized City

ON THE DAY in 1953 when Fred Gardiner took control of the Municipality of Metropolitan Toronto and became the most powerful local politician in the city's history, there was one thing he knew he had to do as soon as possible: build an expressway across the bottom of the city. A few years later he was so proud of his new road, the first urban highway in Canada, that he made it his personal monument. At the time, most of his fellow Torontonians agreed that it was a good symbol of the new era. But one generation's dream can be another's nightmare, and four decades later his accomplishment attracts far more criticism than praise. There are those who would even like to tear the damn thing down.

The Frederick G. Gardiner Expressway has in recent years become the most intractable problem facing anyone who wants to bring new life to the Toronto waterfront. It's the largest piece of urban furniture in the city, bigger by far than the CN Tower or the SkyDome, and its enemies see it as a blight on the cityscape. Even more than the railroad tracks, it cuts off the southern end of Toronto and creates a barrier, both visual and psychological, between Lake Ontario and everything else. But as the friends of the Gardiner point out, it's also essential. We may not like living with it, but we can hardly imagine living without it. In 1992 the planning commissioner of Metro produced a report proving once again, to his satisfaction, that we will need the Gardiner for a long time. Replacing it with an ordinary grade-level road, complete with stoplights, would slow traffic to a pace many people would find intolerable.

Even those who aren't among the 100,000 Gardiner commuters take its convenience for granted. Michael Valpy of *The Globe and Mail* symbolizes the conundrum of Gardiner users who are also Gardiner haters. His column expresses his dislike for the Gardiner, and for what cars have done to Toronto elsewhere. But on days when he leaves from the *Globe* office on Front Street for his country place, he turns onto the Spadina Avenue ramp and sails westward on the Gardiner to Highway 427. He's not a hypocrite: he's an embodiment of the Gardiner dilemma, which will be an issue well into the next century.

Valpy represents the Toronto of today, just as Fred Gardiner represented the Toronto of his day. Valpy's generation wants the city to be big, rich, and humane. Gardiner's generation merely wanted it to be big and rich. Economic growth was the main reason Fred Gardiner's friend and fellow Tory, Premier Leslie Frost, created a new level of government, the Municipality of Metropolitan Toronto, and it was also the reason he chose Gardiner as the first chairman, the "Metro mayor." Gardiner was a fifty-eight-year-old Bay Street lawyer who had served in his spare time as the reeve of Forest Hill Village, a separate municipality in those days. He brought to the Metro job a successful businessman's unshakable confidence, a backroom politician's knack for dealmaking, and an old Tory's view of government as a support system for private business. Gardiner believed that Toronto deserved what he called maximum development, and in his eight years as chairman he did everything he could to make the city larger and wealthier.

He also made municipal politics more abstract, more bureaucratic, and more distant – so distant, in fact, that it baffled the citizens. From the beginning, only a minority of the people understood what the two levels of local government did. Which function was Metro's, and which belonged to Toronto or to suburbs such as Scarborough or North York? You had to follow closely to know – and, just to make it harder, in the early days

Metro was slowly taking over more responsibilities, so the line between the two levels kept changing. This was a time when politicians and town planners liked to preach that municipal government was more important than the provincial or federal levels because it was closer to the public. The public, alas, never learned to see it that way. Voters found that four levels of government were at least one too many to follow, and most of them quietly gave up. Local politics became something to watch occasionally on television rather than a part of daily life. After a while, people thought about municipal government only when it impinged on their personal interests – when an offensively large apartment building was proposed in their neighbourhood, for instance, or taxes rose dramatically.

By the 1970s, most potential voters didn't vote; in a good year the total number of ballots cast was somewhere between 30 and 40 per cent of the number on the voting rolls, and in some municipalities it often fell to the 20s. That gave an edge of irony to the term "popular vote," even though, in the same era that gave us Metro, the right to vote in local elections was extended to include not just property owners but all residents. More complexities lie in the near future. Recently, urban population has reached far beyond Metro's boundaries, and the late 1990s may produce a still larger skeleton of government, for the Greater Toronto Area (GTA). If that happens, many citizens will have lived right through the Metro era without ever having known what it was all about.

Gardiner's own position made Toronto's claim to be a democracy dubious. He was the undisputed boss of major development, but, once his days as Forest Hill reeve were over, he never had to ask the voters for their approval. He was elected to his job by members of Metro council. In the physical building of Toronto he played roughly the same role played in New York for many years by Robert Moses, another appointed politician of great power.

This complicated political machinery may, however, have been necessary. For decades it seemed to work, at the fundamental level of organizing sewers, police, public transit, and arterial roads. And it did so without destroying the egos and jobs of suburban politicians, who were in a position to make a great deal of trouble if their wishes were ignored. Gardiner did not invent Metro government, but he helped to create its structure and he quickly became its personal embodiment. In time, almost everyone agreed that it could not have worked without him.

At Metro, Gardiner found his vocation. He liked big solutions to big problems, and he brought an entrepreneur's energy to local affairs. He loved building things, loved to get plans pushed through and shovels in the ground. Ron Haggart, the leading City Hall columnist of that period, said that what Gardiner ran was less a government than a construction company. It was a comment Gardiner probably didn't regard as an insult. "A municipality is no different from an industrial undertaking," he once said.

That was an outlandish remark – how many industrial undertakings can levy taxes? But in setting up his government, Gardiner had the freedom that owners of new private businesses take for granted. Unlike every other major Canadian politician in this century, he was able to start from scratch. He filled the senior civil service with superb professionals, people he personally chose, who could find persuasive reasons for doing what Gardiner knew needed to be done. In his day Metro was that rare thing, a government without bureaucratic deadwood.

WHEN FRED GARDINER took office, Toronto's path to the future was blocked. The city required many things, including enormous sewer and water systems for the suburbs, but what it most obviously needed was a way of getting tens of thousands of people from the western suburbs into the city each morning and home at night. One of the stars of Gardiner's staff was Sam Cass, a traffic engineer who was much admired in Los Angeles and other expressway-building cities. In 1993, Cass recalled what west Toronto traffic was like in the pre-Metro era: "You didn't have to be a genius to go down there to the Lakeshore and see the need. It was terrible. Whatever we have in the way of congestion now is child's play. Queen and King were just chock-a-block, constantly." A newspaper story called it the most heavily traveled route in Canada.

The solution was as obvious as the problem. North America was in love with automobiles, and people assumed they had a right to commute in their cars. Years before the creation of Metro, the Toronto and York Roads Commission (which Gardiner chaired for a time) had called for a lakeshore highway. The route was a subject of dispute (at one point it was to run south of the Canadian National Exhibition), but the need for it was rarely questioned; hardly anyone suggested that better train service might be the answer. Fifteen years later the anti-expressway movement stopped the Spadina Expressway and ended expressway-building for at least a generation, but no such movement existed in the 1950s. In those days traffic engineers spoke happily of many expressways to come, including one that would have gone just below the Scarborough Bluffs and another that would have sliced through the core of the city, across Davenport Avenue.

So no one was surprised when, just three months after Metro was founded, its council approved the waterfront expressway in principle. The following year, 1954, council approved the western and eastern sections, after Gardiner said that the final design of the central section could wait until "actual traffic using the expressway demonstrates which course is best to follow." The projected cost looked daunting to the councilors, and they knew that any route through the city would meet at least some resistance. So they approved the early stages first, aware all along that, by building the eastern and western ends, they made the central section inevitable.

On May 3, 1954, the day Metro announced the plans, a front-page story in the Toronto *Telegram* reflected that era's affection for high-speed personal travel: "How would you like to drive through Toronto during rush-hour at 50 miles an hour? . . . you would have no stoplights to contend with, no billboards to distract your attention, and no obstacle course of bottlenecks to . . . fray your temper. In addition, you would have a beautiful view of the lake through most of the ten-mile trip, with miles of six-lane, gently curving landscaped highway stretching out in front of you." This miracle, the *Tely* said, would come to pass within four years if the new expressway, "long the collective dream of a few far-sighted planners," received early approval. That piece was typical boosterism of the period. In the 1950s it was commonplace for reporters to believe the drawings put before them by engineers. They even believed politicians. Today the line about billboards has a particularly ironic ring. On the Gardiner westbound, some drivers are grateful for billboards: on a boring and depressing highway, they are the chief visual entertainment.

Work began on the expressway in 1955. It wasn't entirely finished until 1966, the year after the New City Hall was opened. Gardiner was by then five years into retirement, but the expressway had been named for him while he was still in office. One day in 1957, when the first section was nearly completed and Toronto was getting used to the sight of a gigantic highway on stilts, the Metro roads and traffic committee recommended that it be named the Frederick G. Gardiner Expressway as "a gesture of our appreciation" for his outstanding leadership. The motion won approval from the executive committee of council (Fred Gardiner, chairman) and then from Metro council (Fred Gardiner, chairman). The official minutes don't record even a gesture of modesty, such as asking someone else to take the chair during the final vote. This display of egomania created no particular stir. After four years, Toronto was accustomed to the excesses of the man who was shaping its future.

FRED GARDINER was like his expressway: big, ugly, aggressive, and effective. He bulled through Toronto, just like his road, brushing aside everyone who threatened to keep him from going where he wanted to go. There has never been a Toronto politician like him. He beat the Metro councilors into submission so often that after a while some of them gave up and voted for just about anything he proposed. He had more than brute political power, though. In 1958, when the expressway was ceremonially named and Metro gave a party for Gardiner and his wife (whom he always called "Mother"), one of the speakers expressed what was by then a widespread view of Gardiner's political abilities: "Watching him at work has been as thrilling as watching a great creative artist," said Philip Givens, an ardent admirer. By then Gardiner had demonstrated that he had the shrewdness needed to orchestrate the fractious local grandees of the Toronto area while satisfying the Ontario Tory politicians who provided the money for his projects.

In person he was an overwhelming human force, and even his chief weakness, whisky, only heightened his displays of will. There had been years during his career as a lawyer when he avoided alcohol entirely, but in the Metro period he was again drinking heavily. The results were publicly evident on the night of February 1, 1956, when he went with members of the Metro roads committee and some reporters to a meeting with an association of motel owners. The owners were afraid that inadequate access to the new expressway would ruin the business of twenty-three motels on the lakeshore west of Toronto. Over dinner the talk was amiable enough, but later in the evening Gardiner's angry, alcohol-fuelled aggression created something close to hysteria. When the waiters removed plates and cutlery from the dinner tables they left behind only one item, Gardiner's coffee cup. For the rest of the meeting he sipped from it, refilling it frequently from a bottle of whisky stashed under the table.

The head of the association, standing in front of a map, noted that the plans called for only a one-lane eastbound highway on Lake Shore Road. "You're wrong," Gardiner said, interrupting him. "It's two lanes." The man politely said *no*, the plan showed only one. Gardiner didn't like being contradicted. "*You're full of wet hay*," he shouted, at the top of his considerable lungs. A few minutes later, realizing he had been wrong, he announced that he'd made a new decision: "If it isn't two, then I'll make it two. I don't care about the present plan."

His style was contagious. For the rest of the evening, following Gardiner's example, men interrupted each other, shouted, sometimes screamed. Even drunk, he could set the tone for sober people. That night he also demonstrated his contempt for those who questioned him. The owner of the Palace Pier dance hall complained that the expressway would involve expropriating some of his land and might harm his business. "Well, what if it does?" Gardiner shouted. "What if we do have to take fourteen feet off the front of your Palace Pier property, *wouldn't that be just too bad?* It would be too bad if you lost a little bit of that property you got for nothing, wouldn't it?" The man from the Palace Pier shouted, "What do you mean 'for nothing'?" Gardiner said, "You know what I mean. I know you got it for nothing. I knew the people who ran it long before you had anything to do with it." He didn't explain further, and the evening roared on. A report of the meeting that I wrote for the next day's *Globe and Mail* carried a headline, "Gardiner, Motel Men Trade Shouts, Charges." I didn't mention liquor, of course. At the time, discussing a politician's alcoholism in a newspaper was unthinkable, even when it clearly distorted his public performance.

On the design of the expressway, Gardiner's opponents defeated him only once. When his engineers announced a plan to put the road straight through Fort York, they enraged people who cared about local history. Gardiner found himself facing a coalition that included the Canadian Legion and the United Empire Loyalist Association. He offered to move the fort to the lakefront, which he claimed would be more appropriate anyway: it was originally built on the water and had been landlocked by the southward expansion of the city into the lake. No, the preservationists said, they wanted it to stay where it was, where history actually happened. Gardiner surrendered, and bent the expressway. But even when he couldn't get his way, he got his revenge. Today Fort York stands isolated in a lonely triangle formed by the railway, Bathurst Street, and the expressway.

ALL GREAT MONUMENTS left by earlier epochs contain enigmas. The mysteries of the Gardiner hardly rival the riddle of the Sphinx, but they puzzle those who use it or just glance at it from time to time:

Why do pieces of the Gardiner keep falling off? Sometimes a large chunk of concrete detaches itself from the structure and falls thirty or forty feet onto Lake Shore Boulevard; more often, the chunk is knocked off by a maintenance crew just before it falls. How can this be? Bridges built by the Romans still stand all over Europe; it seems preposterous that a road finished in 1966 should self-destruct. The reason is the effect of salt on structural steel, a problem the Romans didn't face because they didn't reinforce their bridges with metal.

Roadsalt makes the Gardiner usable in winter, but eats away at it. Melting snow forms a brine, which flows down through cracks in the concrete. It corrodes the reinforcing steel bars, and the bars eventually swell to as much as ten times their original size. Because rust never sleeps, the Gardiner is never at rest – rust constantly attacks the steel in the structure of the Gardiner (and of many parking garages and bridges built in the same era). This produces an irresistible force, which eventually pushes a chunk of concrete out of its way. Engineers didn't foresee this when the Gardiner was built; now they use steel bars wrapped in epoxy, which cost about twice as much but should last far longer. They have also sealed up some open expansion joints, so at many places the brine now flows down to the drainage system rather than seeping into the structure.

Why does the underside of the Gardiner look diseased? Blotches are the dominating visual characteristic of the Gardiner to anyone who drives under it. Each of them indicates a place where a chunk of concrete dropped off and the space was filled by a primitive concrete technique called "shotcrete." In recent years a neater system has been adopted, and the skin of the Gardiner will eventually look somewhat less scabrous.

What caused the bump on the Humber Bridge? Crossing the Humber, drivers expecting only the usual thrum-thrum of metal stripping beneath their cars suddenly experience a violent whoop, a bit like a roller-coaster ride. Sam Cass has explained why: the bridge, like all the elevated sections of the Gardiner, is "almost a living thing. It moves. It expands and contracts." The problem at the Humber is that the subsoil beside the river wasn't strong enough to hold the bridge. "They should have gone down to bedrock, but they didn't. If you don't have enough money, you cut corners." Over the years, one side has been settling, slowly changing the bridge's shape. The irregularity is no bigger than a speed-bump on a residential street, but at expressway speed it comes as a shock.

Why, on the Gardiner, can't you pull off to the side? There's no shoulder on most of the Gardiner, a fact that terrifies many newcomers to the city. If your car dies, so does your entire lane of traffic, and if your radio is still working you may hear someone in a helicopter reporting to the world that you're stalling traffic on the Gardiner eastbound. If there's an accident, of course, it takes more than the normal time for an ambulance to reach the scene. Metro could have built the Gardiner fourteen feet wider and provided a shoulder on each side. It was cheaper not to.

Why do they keep closing the Gardiner for repairs? In winter the Toronto temperature often jumps back and forth across the freezing point, so the concrete expands and contracts, causing cracks. In the early 1980s it became clear that the Gardiner needed serious help, and in 1984 a major repair program began. It's been running ever since, at a cost of $8 million or so a year. As the Metro engineers see it, the repairs aren't nearly as bothersome as the public believes. Mike Chung, who directs the repairs, claims "Torontonians are very spoiled. They don't like potholes but they don't like traffic disruptions either. One way or another, you have to suffer some inconvenience." On about four weekends each summer, 100 or so workers go up onto the Gardiner at about 9 P.M. Friday; sometimes work is still going on at 5 A.M. Monday. They do some work on week nights, but when the Toronto Blue Jays are in town, Chung says, "They don't like us going up there before midnight," which doesn't leave a lot of working time before they have to get out of the way of the six A.M. traffic. Chung's twenty-year repair program should end in the year 2004, assuming that the expressway is still there. Then the repairs will start all over again.

AT ST. CATHARINES, Ontario, on June 7, 1939, King George VI and Queen Elizabeth officially opened a road named in her honour, the Queen Elizabeth Way, nowadays always shortened to "the QEW." It eventually stretched from Niagara Falls to Toronto, the first four-lane, controlled-access highway in Canada. It was wonderfully fast, but what seems strange today is that it was also charming. The provincial minister of highways, T. B. McQuesten, believed that an important highway should be elegant as well as efficient. In the building of the QEW he used not only highway engineers but also architects, landscape architects, and sculptors. At the gate to Toronto he built a forty-foot-high triumphal column with an enormous British stone lion by the well-known Toronto sculptor Frances Loring at the base. He decorated the bridge at St. Catharines with the crests of the (then) nine provinces.

Today the Gardiner connects with the QEW west of the Humber River, and only the road signs tell drivers they are leaving one era's expressway for another era's highway. The road widenings of the last forty-five years have largely demolished McQuesten's bridges, lighting fixtures, and roadside plantings (Loring's lion ended up in Gzowski Park at the western end of the Gardiner) but in the 1940s the QEW had its own distinct look, connected to Canadian history: it was a specific someplace rather than a generalized noplace. One of its purposes was to make Ontario more accessible to American tourists, and the QEW itself became an attraction. People sometimes used it just for the pleasure of driving on such a beautiful road.

The QEW of the 1930s and the Gardiner of the 1950s, though they were built close to each other in time, nevertheless represent startlingly different ways of life. If you knew nothing about Ontario except those two roads, you might assume that the civilized people who lived there in the 1930s were wiped out and replaced by a race of brutes. The Gardiner has no local character and makes no attempt to be beautiful. It says: I'll get you there faster, don't ask for anything else.

When they built the expressway, and carried out most of the other major projects of the early Metro years, Fred Gardiner and his allies were playing their part in one of the great dramas of urban history, the transformation of the North American city from a single unit into a loose confederation of specialized regions linked by highways. The old-style city placed the various activities of the people close together, but the new, post-1945 confederation separated them. This was the moment when city builders embraced the modern ideal of specialization and tried to make urban planning as rational as manufacturing.

Separating every task into its component parts is the core idea of technology. Most of the great achievements of the century, from automobiles to surgery, would be impossible without it. Even in urban planning, specialization brought certain benefits. It made some of the work of building cities faster and more efficient: houses could be constructed much more quickly when a large tract of land was devoted to nothing else. In general, however, the effect of specialization was deadening. It eliminated spontaneity, and swept aside the individual, small-scale enterprise that made cities exciting.

Among the many activities specialization limited and pigeonholed were traffic engineering and road building. In these fields, as in many others, style and charm surrendered to a glum functionalism. The world wanted so much from the engineers, so fast, that they were forced to abandon beauty and think of nothing but utility. Where once they felt a kinship with architects, they now fell into the same category as sanitary engineers. If we asked sanitary engineers to make their sewers express "a sense of place," they would rightly think us mad. Highway engineers unthinkingly developed the same single-minded commitment to efficiency, and to the belief that everything in nature must surrender to improved communication. All else was sentimentality, and therefore discarded.

Specialization is the signature of modernity. The philosopher Martin Heidegger chose the fate of the Rhine River to symbolize it. The Rhine was once a source of romance and poetry, a place for dreaming as well as fishing and swimming; but modern Europe reduced it to a source of hydroelectric power – "What the river is now, namely, a water-power supplier, derives from the essence of the power station," Heidegger wrote. As J. S. Porter of McMaster University paraphrased him: "A multidimensional reality has been reduced to one dimension. What once was open to a thicket of interpretations shrivels into one interpretation. The river now is what it is used for, no more, no less. We define by utility." Agriculture, rationalized, becomes the food industry, and nature itself "a gigantic gasoline station."

The Gardiner brought specialization to Toronto's lakeshore. For generations the waterfront had been used for work, play, and, of course, transport: Lake Shore Boulevard ran along the water, and the railroad went into the harbour to connect with lake boats. These elements remained more or less in balance until the 1950s, but the Gardiner was built on a scale so overpowering that it made everything else marginal. It transformed an enormous part of the waterfront area into a transmission belt for cars. It destroyed Sunnyside Beach Amusement Park, blocked off the Canadian National Exhibition (which has been in decline ever since), and cast a shadow over dozens of downtown streets. After the Gardiner went up, it continued to thwart some fairly ambitious attempts to use the lakefront for recreation. Ontario Place, the modernist pleasure park on the lake, has been a victim of the Gardiner ever since it opened in 1971: ironically, it's surrounded by transportation (the expressway and the railroad) but remains hard to reach. The Martin Goodman Trail for joggers and cyclists is darkened by what passes overhead.

The Gardiner and the old railroad bridges together produce a forbidding atmosphere. To walk south on York from Front to Queen's Quay on the waterfront is to experience the automobile age at its most oppressive. You pick your way across a series of crossings, some of them made more dangerous by the fact that drivers coming down from the Gardiner, or going up to it, are preoccupied with negotiating the ramps. The Gardiner also destroyed southern Yonge Street, changing it from an urban street into an adjunct of the traffic system. Walking down Yonge to the *Star* building, you are made to feel that your presence as a pedestrian is barely tolerated.

Still, the Gardiner hasn't kept the waterfront from becoming a popular site for development. The federal government, by creating the Harbourfront Corporation in the early 1970s, started the process of regeneration and in 1975 the appearance of the Harbour Castle Hotel (now the Westin Harbour Castle) demonstrated that the waterfront held commercial possibilities. The Harbourfront Corporation put $30 million into capital works, and soon there were marinas, restaurants, art galleries, pubs, a couple of theatres, an antique market, and about 3 million visitors a year. Harbourfront Centre was (and is) chaotic, but alive – though 1995 cutbacks in funds provided by Ottawa threatened its existence. The 1980s development boom brought a condominium building designed by Arthur Erickson, the warehouse renovation (apartments, stores, offices, another theatre) by Eberhard Zeidler called Queen's Quay – and more boring apartment buildings than anyone cared to contemplate. Today the Gardiner still looms over everything, its up-on-stilts traffic roaring along, but the waterfront is a long way from dead.

Then why try to change the Gardiner? The people who built it fail to see the point. As Sam Cass has said, "You have something workable now, and if you change it you will also have something workable, after spending a lot more money." Cass doubts that the problem of the Gardiner-as-barrier will be solved; he thinks that almost any ambitious plan (turning part of the Gardiner into a tunnel, for instance) will likely have to be paid for, at least in part, by putting new buildings on the land on which the Gardiner now sits. Those new structures will also cut off the waterfront, he argues – though they will do it in a different way and will be designed in a period (unlike the 1950s) when people see the waterfront as an asset.

In the 1980s a developer, William Teron, offered to pay the titanic cost of burying the Gardiner under Toronto Island, in return for large chunks of Gardiner land. If another property boom ever materializes, similar ideas will appear. A less ambitious but still hugely expensive plan might bring the Gardiner down to grade level from, say, Spadina Avenue to just east of Yonge Street, letting the rest of it stand as it is. Downtown could then acquire a grand boulevard in place of an eyesore. It would be slower but prettier; in theory, property values would increase enough to pay the cost. Downtown would be integrated, the city put in touch with its lake.

This is among many ideas generated by the waterfront commission under David Crombie's leadership. The most popular mayor of Toronto in generations, he was brought back from federal to local politics by the pressing problems of the lakefront. Crombie had come to public life in the 1960s from his job as a political science teacher at Ryerson Institute of Technology in downtown Toronto, and for years he had been the political embodiment of the city's best hopes for itself. When he was mayor, his home number appeared in the telephone book under "Crombie, Mayor David," and he accepted the annoyance of 150 phone calls a week from strangers because he wanted to live in a city where the mayor was just another citizen. He was an opponent of over-specialized development, a passionate advocate of old neighbourhoods, but no radical; he belonged to the Progressive Conservative Party's Red Tory wing. Radicals on council, though they sometimes worked with him, viewed his popularity with suspicion and a certain resentment.

He had the natural politician's ability to make his own ideas look like consensus, and he could pull together the votes of reformers and "old guard" members of council better than anyone else in recent times. He was comfortable with dealmaking, and he approached land developers with an optimistic good humour that served both him and the city well. After two successful terms as mayor, from 1973 to 1978, he represented Rosedale in the federal parliament, ran unsuccessfully for national leader of the Conservatives, and served as a cabinet minister under two prime ministers, Joe Clark and Brian Mulroney.

After an ugly row of apartment buildings appeared along the waterfront in the 1980s, it began to look as if Toronto was squandering another chance to make the downtown lakeshore inviting. In 1988 the federal government assigned Crombie to run the Royal Commission on the Future of the Toronto Waterfront. Four years later that turned into the Waterfront Regeneration Trust, an Ontario agency with Crombie as director. He set out to find ideas to improve the waterfront and bring together the governments and corporations that would make them work. And that of course brought him up against the Gardiner Expressway, whose most persistent critic he soon became.

Crombie has always found this part of his work frustrating. As soon as someone starts talking about changing the Gardiner, the Metro government announces that it's absolutely essential and nothing can be done about it. It's hard to get the debate going. As Crombie has said, "The debate so far has been – you can do anything you want to the shoreline, and ruin the lake if you like, but don't touch the Gardiner. It's part of our nervous system." While he wants to create public discussion, he avoids framing the argument as a struggle between bicycle-riding car haters and those who believe the private automobile is essential to civilization. He doesn't want Toronto to find itself deciding whether to tear down the Gardiner or leave it untouched. He knows his side would lose.

Still, the Gardiner as it stands is an abomination. What's to be done with it? Crombie thinks we may end up cutting part of it into the ground and covering it over, building on top of the tunnel we create. He also believes that improved public transit from the west and improved local roads will make the Gardiner less vital and make a change more attractive. But there's no one Crombie Plan for the Gardiner, and he acknowledges that it may have to be changed bit by bit, over twenty years or so. He hopes to redress the balance that was destroyed in the 1950s, turn that section of Toronto from a corridor into a place where people live, work, and play. "I'd like to see it integrated into the urban fabric of Toronto." Such a simple idea. Such an enormous task. No matter what Toronto decides to do, it will be prodigiously difficult. It will probably require the skills of a politician as powerful and shrewd as Fred Gardiner.

NO SUCH POLITICIAN has appeared, and perhaps a career like Gardiner's would be impossible now: the tangle of interests that political leaders confront in the 1990s is far more complicated than it was in the 1950s. It seems likelier that changes in city planning will be produced not by powerful leaders but by social forces largely beyond the control of politicians. One such force is slowly undermining the principle of segregated planning that was considered an unassailable truth in Gardiner's day.

If you drive north on the Allen Expressway and keep going for eight or ten kilometres after it turns into Dufferin Street, past Finch Avenue and then Steeles Avenue, perhaps as far north as Rutherford Road, you begin to understand the term "leapfrog development." It means dropping isolated pockets of humanity more or less at random into a vast, mainly empty landscape. This sparsely occupied strip provides a good place to think about the future development of Toronto, and moving through it in a car may be the right way to stimulate that thinking. The automobile, after all, made the landscape of Dufferin Street possible. As a 1991 report to the Metropolitan Toronto government put it: "By dramatically improving mobility, the automobile... permitted vast new areas of land to be developed. Development could 'leapfrog' open areas.... The pressure for compact, denser forms of development was removed, and low-density, suburban forms began to dominate." That three-sentence history describes the hop-and-skip process of urban expansion that the Toronto region has lived through for forty years, and Dufferin graphically illustrates it. More important, these recurring empty spaces raise an issue that should dominate the debate over the future shape of Toronto: the question of density.

Driving north on Dufferin you pass houses, a school, maybe a church, and then for a while nothing but empty fields or an abandoned factory, then another clump of houses. This form of civilization is neither urban nor suburban, nor is it rural: it's a meandering extension of the city through a scarred remnant of the country. When you pass Steeles you officially leave Metro, but borders don't mean much here. Politicians take boundaries seriously, and even attach the preposterous word "city" to suburbs that aren't. Most residents say they live in Toronto.

The real Toronto, that is; not the nineteenth century incorporated city or the Municipality of Metropolitan Toronto but the gigantic agglomeration that grows in the haphazard style of Dufferin Street. This is the social geography of the automobile age, Toronto as designed by General Motors and Nissan. But

while the automobile has influenced city planning more profoundly than anything since the invention of fortified towns, it's
only one of two forces that created the phenomenon represented
by Dufferin. The other is a perverse ideology that sees the city
as a necessary evil and the suburbs as the natural home of peace,
freedom, and healthy families. Harley Sherlock, a British
architect and advocate of higher densities, titled his book on the
subject *Cities Are Good For Us*. In the context of residential
construction during the second half of the century, that's an
almost defiant statement.

In the 1950s North American society began developing controlled communities that differed sharply from traditional cities;
in Toronto the new era began with Don Mills in 1952. We made,
without much public discussion, a momentous decision. For
the first time in the history of human settlement, we decided to
separate the activities of life and assign to each piece of land a
specialized function. Work would go here, housing there, and
shopping there. In pre-1952 Toronto, as in traditional European
cities, it was normal for people to live a short distance from
where they worked, so that getting them to and from the job was
not the expensive project it is today. Now only about a fifth of
all the land in Metropolitan Toronto mixes work and housing.
The rest is rigidly segregated.

For many years, this radical new arrangement looked to most
people like the natural evolution of cities. Those who considered
it alienating were a minority. After about twenty years, however, one unfortunate result became evident across the continent:
chronic air pollution caused by millions of automobiles used for
long periods twice a day. This became a public issue in the 1970s.
Over the years since, environmentalism has often appeared to be
a movement of genuine power. But no matter how strong it
becomes, it never affects city planning in a noticeable way. So
far, we have placed our belief in freedom of choice ahead of our
concern about the environment.

Scattered growth theoretically could have gone on forever,
but in the early 1990s a new force emerged. Apparently it's more
significant than environmentalism and just as powerful and

unstoppable as the technological and cultural influences that created contemporary Toronto. The new force is public debt. The realization of how much money we owe (and will continue to owe, for as long as anyone now living remains on earth) has reorganized our most fundamental ideas about government. It has turned social democrats into conservatives and put every public expenditure under intense scrutiny. At the level of town planning, it has imposed a terrifying new discipline on local councils. Dimly, we now understand that the creation of Dufferin Street, and the other corridors that resemble it, was fabulously expensive. Those are luxuries we can no longer afford.

On the surface, the spread of Toronto looked like the work of private enterprise. Corporations put up houses and apartment buildings to be bought or rented by private citizens. But every extension of the city also cost great sums of public money. Local governments, heavily backed by Ontario, had to race after the private developers, laying down roads and water and sewer pipes, building schools and transit systems. Because they were in the business of issuing or not issuing the permits for construction, local councils sometimes looked like an obstruction to development. In fact, they were essential to it. They and the land developers formed an alliance whose purpose was to create and sell new living space.

Behind all this, along with normal commercial motives, was an impulse that reached deeply into North American thinking and touched everything we did: the natural human desire for freedom. The new suburbs offered the citizens more control over where and how they lived. Citizens acquired freedom as house buyers, shoppers, and car owners. Many acquired unprecedented amounts of privately owned space. These are not insignificant factors, and intellectuals who casually deride the suburbs fail to understand that in many ways they respond to human aspiration. Critics who see the creation of the suburbs as a kind of conspiracy between land developers and politicians, and see suburbanites as victims, fail to notice that many people who can afford to live anywhere choose to live in the suburbs.

But what was good for consumers (at least some of them) was not so good for taxpayers. Consumers were enriched by new freedoms, but as taxpayers they had to accept huge costs. At every turn the public either put out large sums of money in taxes or borrowed against the future. And the more our communities spread, the more money we wasted. Sewer pipes that pass beneath thinly populated districts, transit lines that remain chronically underused, local roads that carry few cars, school buses that must drive farther and farther to pick up their passengers, school buildings that are abandoned as their districts go out of fashion while other districts furiously throw money into new schools: each of these represents substantial waste.

For many years we accepted these public costs, because endless economic growth was taken for granted and the development of even a scattered new suburb looked like a sound investment in the future. In retrospect it seems to have been a wonderful, dream-like time. But no one holds those beliefs anymore, and finally a new law of planning has emerged: low density means high cost. A second rule follows automatically: all this has to stop. Cities, if they are to use their resources economically, must become more city-like.

The Reurbanisation of Metropolitan Toronto, a two-volume study prepared for the Metro government by the planning firm of Berridge Lewinberg Greenberg, argues that by careful use of resources Metro can accommodate any imaginable growth in population (the highest estimate for the next twenty to thirty years is 500,000 new jobs and 800,000 new residents) without building expensive new roads or transit lines and without eating up more farmland. Within Metro itself "there is a wealth of places in which reurbanisation can occur."

"Reurbanisation" describes the process that planners have been trying to set in motion. ("Intensification" is another term.) The reurbanisation report was one sign of this movement. Another is the Toronto planning department's recent attempt, so far unsuccessful, to intensify development through its Housing on Main Streets program, which would change the rules to permit five-storey apartment buildings above stores on major streets, like St. Clair, Queen, and the Danforth. The careful attention paid to this issue by the Ontario government's Commission on Planning and Development Reform, chaired by

John Sewell in the early 1990s, was another sign of change. The commission made urban intensification seem both necessary and inevitable. In the future outlined by Sewell and his colleagues, "Communities will be planned to minimize the consumption of land" and promote efficient use of sewers, water supplies, transit systems, and other services already in place. Local zoning by-laws will encourage intensification in carefully chosen built-up areas.

Planners focusing on this issue aren't alone. Many politicians and developers also recognize the need to use existing resources rather than creating new ones with borrowed money. But almost all agree that the idea still meets stiff public resistance. And no wonder: intensification demands nothing less than a 180-degree change in public attitudes. After all, for decades "high density" was precisely what was wrong with cities; "teeming," often used in conjunction with "tenements," was the word that expressed the distaste of those who believed that packed city streets bred crime, disease, and ignorance. The war on high density was a major reason for the creation of city planning as a profession; planners wrote laws to cut density, or limit it. Now the same profession must tell the public that we need more density. This may not be as hard as, say, convincing Russians that private business is both good and necessary, but it's that kind of fundamental change.

Cultural bias is the emotional subtext to the public drama of urban development. Since the Industrial Revolution, the weight of culture has supported the idea that the country is beautiful and virtuous, the city ugly and evil. The great poets of the countryside, from William Wordsworth to Robert Frost, affirm life; the great city poets, from Charles Baudelaire to T. S. Eliot, specialize in depravity, bleakness, and despair. Journalism, particularly as it reflects American experience, has so reinforced the idea of "inner city crime" that Toronto newspapers sometimes refer to "the problems of the inner city" when they are in fact talking about something that is literally in the suburbs. As John Sewell says, "To reverse the cultural bias of one hundred years will take some time."

Even so, there is no avoiding it. If the Toronto region acquires a few hundred thousand new residents in the next generation, the only practical course is to fit them within the urban fabric that now exists. Among other things, intensification will mean building on abandoned industrial land. The Toronto region has enough obsolete industrial sites to keep developers busy for most of the next century. Infill developments in established districts will provide more space, when we overcome our fear that any increase in density will bring a street-clogging flood of cars. And municipal governments (such as Scarborough's), will come to their senses and recognize that the thousands of illegal basement apartments now existing in what are officially "single-family dwellings" are in fact logical and harmless ways of using those houses, a reflection of changes in styles of family life. They should be made legal and therefore more attractive.

But the fundamental decisions will be made, as always, by individuals. While planners and politicians imagine they're responsible for creating cities, human settlement moves forward partly by accident and partly through the minute choices made by individuals. Where to live, where to pray, where to shop, where to attend school, how to spend spare time: when we make these choices we are all town planners. What we now have to bear in mind is that the rules have radically changed, just as they did forty years ago at the dawn of the age of the suburb, when Fred Gardiner saw the future and made it his.

5

Ballet of the Streets

ONE OF THE REMARKABLE THINGS about the St. Lawrence Neighbourhood, in the south-east corner of central Toronto, is that hardly anyone finds it remarkable. It is the largest downtown housing development built in North America in this century, it was put there only two decades ago, and it's not hidden. It begins at the city core, right behind the O'Keefe Centre for the Performing Arts, and runs east to Parliament Street. It is a big, government-organized scheme that actually works – something as rare in land development as in any other field. And, while it exists right beside the Gardiner Expressway, it embodies a philosophy that is opposed to everything the Gardiner represents.

Yet when we talk about the major events in recent Toronto history, we rarely mention the St. Lawrence Neighbourhood. Even when we speak nostalgically of 1970s reform politics, we focus on other achievements. Most of these tend to be negative, the avoidance of this or that, the saving of something. The defeat of the Spadina Expressway remains the most famous victory: that gigantic road would have ripped through much of west-central Toronto in the early 1970s if it hadn't been cancelled by a coalition of reform politicians, local property owners, artists, and an Ontario government that was about to face an election. The stopping of big, intrusive apartment developments in old residential districts has also been celebrated. But the St. Lawrence Neighbourhood was the tour de force of the reform era, proof that on at least one occasion the reformers could deliver on their promise of a more liveable city. It is the chief monument of David Crombie's time as mayor; appropriately, part of it is named for him. It demonstrates what local government can, on its best days, accomplish.

In retrospect, it seems almost miraculous that it was built at all. A plan of this size would be hard to execute at any time, but the atmosphere of the mid-1970s made it especially daunting. A cloud of failure had gathered over the very idea of government housing. In Britain, the new towns planned with supreme confidence in the 1940s and 1950s had turned out to be disappointments at best, calamities at worst. The politicians eagerly embraced the worst ideas of planners – plain, high buildings set in what were intended to be large parks. The Labour Party of Glasgow campaigned for re-election in 1970 by boasting that it had built the highest council-flats buildings in Europe; they were thirty-one storeys, and they were later regarded as a major mistake. Michael Ignatieff has argued that the failure of social democracy in Britain was, above all, an architectural failure – the vast acres of council flats were the most visible signs of Labour Party achievement, and they impressed neither their residents nor the middle-class voters whose taxes helped pay for them. In the United States, the results of planning were even worse: housing projects in Detroit, Chicago, and many other cities had become zones of terror.

By the mid-1970s, hardly anyone had a good word to say for Regent Park, the public housing project that had replaced a few blocks of downtown Toronto slums in the 1950s. The architects and planners, following modernist principles set down by Le Corbusier and others, bulldozed the old city streets and created enclaves, isolating Regent Park from the city around it. Like many of the projects now run by the Metropolitan Toronto Housing Authority, Regent Park was laid out on the principle that people living in it could be protected from social infection if they were physically separated from the old, unredeemed slums that continued to exist nearby. In the beginning, many of the developments were regarded as efficient and humane – in

1958 the maisonette towers of Regent Park South won national recognition in the form of a Massey Medal for Peter Dickinson, one of the most admired Toronto architects of the day.

Later, the reputation of the projects faded and then grew sinister. Planned with the highest hopes, they bred despair. By setting themselves apart, they loudly announced that their residents were second-class citizens. And the squares and parks at the centre of the projects – Dickinson was especially proud of the open space in Regent Park South – became glaring symbols of failure. In architects' drawings they looked attractive, but they turned out to be lifeless wasteland, which no one wanted to use or care for. Public-housing tended to be inconvenient as well. Shopping was usually kept at a distance from the apartments, and entrances were hard to reach by ambulance, taxi, or delivery truck. Today the only people who find Regent Park entirely congenial are drug dealers, who can hide there with more ease than on ordinary streets. Most dealers live elsewhere, but they come to do business in the neglected hallways and entrances, bringing violence with them.

In the 1970s this was the familiar reality of government housing everywhere. In Toronto, politicians and planners had a special reason for trepidation. Living among them, and already a good friend to several of them, was the most famous analyst of gigantic urban mistakes, Jane Jacobs. She had moved to Toronto from New York in the late 1960s, and her presence in the city was a nagging reminder that intelligent, well-meaning people can get everything horribly wrong.

THE ARRIVAL OF Jane Jacobs, though uncelebrated at the time, was one of the happiest accidents in Toronto history. In the late 1960s she and her husband left New York because they found America in the Vietnam era oppressive – and because they had two draft-age sons. They could have chosen any city, but they picked Toronto because it seemed an agreeable place and there was work for Bob Jacobs as an architect.

The reputation of Jane Jacobs arrived well ahead of her. Anyone interested in city building knew about her first book,

The Death and Life of Great American Cities, a merciless critique of the barren new districts created by the overweening ambition of planners – and of the theories standing behind those planners. The book was much discussed in Toronto, as elsewhere; before it was a year old, teachers were referring to it in the University of Toronto town planning course. Eberhard Zeidler, whose architectural firm hired Bob Jacobs, has described the book's effect on him: "It was as if somebody had torn blindfolds from my eyes." But her presence in the city turned out to be even more significant than anyone might have expected.

Jacobs began taking part in events connected with city politics, from public demonstrations to hearings of the Ontario Municipal Board, and sometimes she affected crucial decisions – as she did in the leadership of the St. Lawrence Neighbourhood. In subtle ways, she became a potent force in city life. Her influence was spread across Toronto by architects, politicians, and journalists she saw privately, people who had been won over by her book and came to her seeking advice or stimulating talk. Beyond question, she brought a message to the city. She understood that ideas rule the world, and she wanted Toronto to sharpen its ideas about itself. She animated the discussion of city-building by placing Toronto's concerns in the context of a long-running international argument about how cities could revive themselves. Jacobs advised her readers to focus on the details of local planning, understand the local context, come up with local solutions. At the same time, this most local of thinkers helped Toronto to see its own problems as a reflection of the state of cities everywhere. She gave Toronto's thoughts about itself an international context.

She was an unlikely intellectual warrior, a theorist who opposed most theories, a teacher with no teaching job and no university degree, a writer who wrote well but infrequently. She was the classic self-taught thinker, one of those people who try to figure everything out for themselves. When she graduated from high school in Scranton, Pennsylvania, she decided that she had endured enough formal education and would learn the rest on her own. She went off to discover the world and herself.

In the middle of the Depression, walking the streets of New York in search of jobs, she became, by accident, a student of the diversity of city life. Slowly she found her subject, and bit by bit she found her theme: cities as organisms that appear chaotic but actually follow their own changing patterns. She worked as a secretary and began to write in her spare time. Many of her early magazine articles were on aspects of city life – articles in *Vogue*, for instance, on the fur district and the diamond district. Once she wrote an article in *Cue* magazine on manhole covers and what they indicate about life beneath the streets. In 1944 she married Robert Hyde Jacobs, and ever since they have developed their ideas together. In the 1950s, working on the staff of *Architectural Forum*, she was assigned to write about hospitals and schools and given a roll of architectural plans to study. At home she asked her husband to explain them. As they studied together, Jane learned about architecture and Bob became so enthralled that he eventually made hospitals his specialty. Since their move to Canada he has worked on major hospitals in Edmonton, Hamilton, and Toronto, among other places.

In the 1950s *Architectural Forum* published optimistic pieces on new housing developments. Jacobs went to see them, analysed them in detail, and discovered something that was fresh news at the time: they weren't working. Planners had bulldozed large slum areas and replaced them with carefully organized collections of apartment buildings and open spaces. On paper they looked fine, but when Jacobs visited them she discovered that the open spaces were empty of people. Planners had segregated residences, retail stores, business offices, and schools, an arrangement that was tidy but also inhuman and uninteresting. Amazingly, people appeared to like these projects less than they had liked the old slums. An environment created out of goodwill and careful thought had turned out to be boring, dangerous, and ultimately unliveable. The new developments had literally been planned to death: they left no room for happy accidents, and no room for life. How could such a thing have happened?

THE FIRST HALF of the 1960s produced a cluster of influential books which looked at old phenomena in new ways. All of them were acts of intrusion on specialized territory by authors who lacked academic credentials. In 1960 Paul Goodman, a poet and playwright, wrote *Growing Up Absurd,* a book about youth and delinquency so startlingly fresh in its insights that it influenced professional educators for decades after. In 1962, Rachel L. Carson, who was mainly a journalist rather than a scientist (though she had a master's degree in marine biology) wrote the book that launched the environmental movement, *Silent Spring,* an attack on the poisoning of nature by insecticides. In 1963 Betty Friedan, a freelance magazine writer, wrote *The Feminine Mystique,* which questioned basic assumptions about the role of women; it started a new wave of feminism and affected the conduct of everyday life more than the work of any professional psychologist or social scientist of the day. In 1964 Marshall McLuhan, an English professor reaching far beyond the confines of his discipline, wrote *Understanding Media,* a landmark in communications studies, so influential that its central ideas became part of the language. And in 1965 a lawyer, Ralph Nader, wrote *Unsafe at Any Speed,* a powerful book about a subject in which he held no credentials, automobile engineering.

All of these outsiders challenged the reigning assumptions of the subjects they dealt with, and all were resisted at first by specialists. In that sense, the Jacobs book was a product of its time, a moment of great hope in America, before the start of the Vietnam War and the souring of public discourse; it appeared in 1961, the first year of John Kennedy's presidency. Of the other books, it most resembled *Silent Spring.* Just as Rachel Carson was principally interested not in pest-killing chemicals but in their effects on the life forms she studied, Jane Jacobs was concerned not so much with planning theory as with the people affected by it. Jacobs depicted cities as intricate working organisms, the way naturalists see ecosystems. *Silent Spring* and *The Death and Life of Great American Cities* can be read side by side as similar commentaries on the hubris of technology.

By the time Jacobs's book appeared, criticism of the big housing developments was spreading; there had already been a few articles on "the new slums." But those who noticed the squalor of public projects assumed that they had failed because they inadequately carried out the noble vision behind them. Jacobs took the opposite tack. The vision was wrong, she said, and it wasn't noble. "This book," Jacobs began, "is an attack on current city planning and rebuilding." She went on to demonstrate that the great planners had become so enraptured by their own dreams of order and beauty that they had failed to notice how people live. Neighbourhoods she said, can be created only out of the common experience of the citizens. They cannot be devised by a central authority. She challenged not simply the mistakes she saw around her but the very notion of a designed urban utopia, an idea to which generations of intellectuals had wistfully committed themselves. For the great movements in town-planning theory, movements that all architects studied in university, she had a startling and contemptuous word – "reactionary."

The reviews of *Death and Life* were mainly positive, sprinkled liberally with words like "richness" and "seminal." But many of the critics who admired the book felt compelled to distance themselves from it. Professionals found it hard to watch Jacobs undermine the social rationale for zoning, the carving up of cities into single-use neighbourhoods. She argued that this idea, the principal activity of city planners, was nonsense, and dangerous nonsense. It was as if she had somehow tried to persuade dentists that filling teeth did more harm than good.

Reviewers found Jacobs overly harsh in the way she dealt with those who were heroes to planners and architects, not only Le Corbusier but also Ebenezer Howard, Sir Patrick Geddes, and even the man regarded as a living saint of urbanism – Lewis Mumford. After the book appeared, Mumford's own response was eagerly awaited. In 1961, at the age of sixty-six, he was an Olympian figure in American culture, the author of grandly ambitious books on city-building and a much-studied column on architecture in *The New Yorker.* He had noted some of Jacobs's earlier work with pleasure and agreement, and perhaps he opened her book in the expectation of agreeing further. Instead he found that the entire Garden City tradition, for which he was the most articulate advocate, was under attack. With astonishment, he read that the Garden City dream of a peaceful, orderly environment for humanity was draining the life from cities. Mumford was irked, and even more irked when he discovered that some reviewers thought Jacobs's ideas made his outdated.

Mumford began composing a reply almost as soon as he closed the book. Later he wrote to a friend, "I held my fire...for a whole year, but when I got down to write I discovered that the paper burned, in spite of the long cooling period." His biographer, Donald L. Miller, tells us that Mumford wrote not one but three long articles. *The New Yorker* persuaded him to cut them to a single piece and tone down his anger. His article, "Mother Jacobs' Home Remedies," running through twenty pages of the December 1, 1962 issue, satirized her ideas: "If people are housed in sufficiently congested quarters – provided only that the buildings are not set within superblocks – and if there is a sufficient mishmash of functions and activities, all her social and aesthetic demands are satisfied." He described her as a writer of some insight who had gone horribly wrong.

Death and Life annoyed Mumford and his sympathizers because of the ferocity and directness with which Jacobs attacked; but her message was not entirely negative. She found a luminous pleasure in city life, the "ballet of the streets." Her celebration of traditional streets as the focus of community life was essentially positive, but it set her against the modernist architectural tradition embodied in the work of Mies van der Rohe and his followers. Modernist architects ignored or erased the streets on which they put their buildings – and in doing so ignored the most vivid and potentially exciting aspect of a city's public life.

Jacobs came down firmly on the side of the spontaneous inventiveness of individuals, as against abstract plans imposed by governments and corporations – an argument she was to make later, in a different way, when she wrote on economics. A theory of social organization, based on the humblest sort of observation, was embedded in her book.

Eventually *Death and Life* reached far beyond planning issues and influenced the spirit of the time. In 1982, in a widely admired book of social theory, *All That Is Solid Melts Into Air,* the New York critic Marshall Berman wrote that Jacobs played "a crucial role in the development of modernism" – the late version of modernism that began emerging in the 1960s and was eventually called "post-modern." She did this, Berman argued, by demonstrating that the meaning for which modern people search lies close to home, in the perpetual motion and change of the city, an "evanescent but intense and complex face-to-face communication and communion."

Peter Blake, who worked with Jacobs on *Architectural Forum* and found her "a wonderfully likeable, contentious, opinionated woman," described the impact of her ideas in his memoirs, *No Place Like Utopia.* In the 1940s and 1950s, he recalled, the great planning schemes of the century, like Le Corbusier's Unité d'Habitation in Marseilles, seemed altogether rational. The central beliefs of modern urbanism were accepted by just about everyone connected with architecture. "Only a very few among us were ready to challenge Le Corbusier's diagrams – and the brightest of these critics, by far, was Jane Jacobs." While other journalists enthusiastically promoted utopian diagrams for urban renewal, Jacobs raised more and more questions – "until, in 1960, she spoke out passionately at an urban design conference at Harvard and challenged virtually all the notions up till then accepted."

When Jacobs put these challenges in her book, she "completely altered the discourse on the nature and future of cities." Blake, a conventional modernist, found her advocacy of a form of creative chaos unsettling. "It took me several years to come to terms with her extraordinary vision of a truly free, egalitarian society...." When a German architect visited Blake in New York, he demanded to meet Jacobs, whose book had created a storm of discussion across Europe; twenty years later, when Blake worked on a major urban renewal project in West Berlin, everyone connected with it was conscious that the ideas of Jacobs were shaping their plans. Jane Jacobs had become a factor in town planning everywhere – and in Toronto most of all.

SHE AND HER FAMILY settled in the Annex, a district that illustrated Jacobsian principles even before she identified them. They bought a house on Albany Avenue. By coincidence, that was the same street where Eric Arthur – the New Zealander whose role as the city's architectural guide and conscience was similar, in earlier decades, to the part Jacobs was to play from the 1970s to the 1990s – had lived with his family in the 1930s.

Within a few years, she became part of Toronto folklore. One story demonstrates not only her views but the vigorous and imaginative ways she put them to work. Like many stories from the period, it concerns a threatened chunk of the architectural past, a row of houses on a street that was splendid through much of the late nineteenth century and squalid through much of the twentieth. In the early 1970s a property developer acquired the right to demolish some worn, old houses on Sherbourne Street, just north of Dundas, and replace them with apartment buildings. When some of the politicians who were trying to save downtown neighbourhoods heard of that decision, they set about getting it reversed. But they were afraid that the houses would be torn down while they were working their way through the bureaucracy, so they planned a protest demonstration.

Early on the cold, dark morning of April 5, 1973, about eighty demonstrators assembled at the site. Among them were Alderman John Sewell, Alderman William Kilbourn, and Jane Jacobs. Once the protesters gathered, they were unsure of what to do. Jacobs heard a lawyer in their group remark thoughtfully that, by law, demolition could proceed only if the houses were enclosed by hoardings, the boards that hide and protect the site. That was all Jacobs needed. She turned to Kilbourn. "They can't do this if the hoardings are down," she announced in her loud, American twang. "Here, give me a hand."

Kilbourn and Jacobs went to work, others joined them, and in no time the hoardings lay on the ground. By the time the wrecking crew arrived, the houses to be demolished stood exposed to the street. Apparently the union agreement did not allow demolition workers to replace the hoardings. The houses were saved for the moment, and that temporary reprieve won by Jacobs and her fellow demonstrators eventually turned into a permanent pardon. The city bought the houses from the developer, restored them, filled in spaces around them with more housing, and created a low-rent development that holds more people than would have lived in the planned apartment buildings. That little strip of history will stand, well into the twenty-first century, as evidence both of Toronto society in the 1870s and of the intense save-our-city politics that developed a century later. When the city builds a monument to Jacobs, it should probably go there.

In September, 1991, to celebrate the thirtieth anniversary of *The Death and Life of Great American Cities,* some of her friends and admirers held a day in her honour. There was a luncheon at the University of Toronto faculty of architecture, in rooms decorated with photographs illustrating quotations from the book; there was a public symposium that went on all afternoon; and finally there was a dinner that lasted late into the evening as architects, planners, politicians, and journalists rose one after another to explain what she had meant in their lives and the life of the city.

Through it all she smiled benignly, a tall, stooped woman with the look of an ancient hawk. As usual, she didn't dress up. She wore to her own party more or less what she wears to everybody else's parties and indeed wears whenever she goes out – a large corduroy tent and running shoes. As usual, she exhibited no sense of her own importance. In 1961 she started a revolution that reached around the world, yet she insists that what she writes is only common sense. Still, it would be as wrong to call her modest as to accuse her of boastfulness. On that occasion, sitting for ten or so hours beneath a shower of undiluted praise, she seemed altogether at ease, as if she could look on her work honestly, objectively, and without false modesty. She appeared to be that rare and enviable creature, an integrated personality; her writing, not her ego, absorbs her.

EVEN SO, HER PRESENCE in Toronto is enough to make any ambitious city planner nervous. Certainly the possibility of failure was in every city planner's mind when the St. Lawrence

Neighbourhood appeared on the agenda in the 1970s. Given the disasters Jacobs had exposed, who in Toronto would have the nerve to propose that the city acquire forty-four acres, a property much bigger than Regent Park, and put 10,000 people on it? At the centre of local government there were two youngish men who possessed sufficient daring. Crombie, an alderman for three years, became mayor in 1973 at the age of thirty-seven. Michael Dennis, a lawyer, served as housing adviser in Crombie's office and became city housing commissioner in 1974, when he was thirty-two. Both of them had large ambitions, some of which were later fulfilled. Both were politically astute. While Crombie became a federal cabinet minister, Dennis turned into a major figure in the international property empire of the Reichmann family. And in the 1970s Crombie had promises to keep. Affordable housing was part of his platform.

The man who directed their attention to the properties south of Front Street, from Yonge to Parliament, was Frank Lewinberg, then on the city planning staff. It was historic land, in a sense. Just to the north, in the late eighteenth century, Governor John Graves Simcoe had laid out York, the first version of Toronto. In those days Front Street was the lakefront; it wasn't until the middle of the nineteenth century that landfill extended the city southward into the lake. Railroad yards and factories kept the new land occupied for generations, but by the 1970s many factories were closed and the landscape was dominated by scrapyards and empty warehouses. It was not an obvious place to put apartment buildings and town houses: the noisy, smelly Gardiner Expressway and the railroad defined the southern border. Nevertheless, Lewinberg suggested that it might be used for housing. He convinced his boss in the planning department, Howard Cohen, and they took it to Dennis and Crombie.

Like everyone else in this story, Dennis knew about the potential for embarrassing, large-scale failure. He also knew that an ambitious and unusual development would not easily be embraced by the bureaucrats at City Hall. He decided to hire an outside planner, and he consulted his neighbour on Albany Avenue, Jane Jacobs. She recommended a young architect, Alan

Littlewood, who had impressed her when he worked with Bob Jacobs on the design of a Detroit hospital. Littlewood had never thought of himself as a town planner, and held no planning degree; that appealed to Jacobs, whose admiration for professional planners remains severely limited. Littlewood took the job, stayed for two years, and wrote the planning specifications, after many discussions with politicians, citizens' groups, and architects; Zeidler drew up preliminary plans (and later designed one of the buildings). When Littlewood left, in 1976, the style of the St. Lawrence Neighbourhood was in place.

Early on, within earshot of Jacobs, Littlewood used the word "project" to describe what he was doing. "Don't do that!" she said. "Don't say *project*." He asked what was wrong with the word. "Say neighbourhood, as in community," Jacobs told him. "The way you think about it will determine what you do." That was typical of Jacobs, who believes that language governs us more than we know. Littlewood saw the point. He began to think of his work as a version of "infill," a relatively new idea then being promoted by a number of architects, notably Jack Diamond. The infill approach fits new housing into established streets without destroying the old environment, sometimes tucking a few apartments or townhouses into empty or badly used spaces in barely noticeable ways. Littlewood calls this "urban dentistry" – or, changing the metaphor, "invisible mending." He decided that the St. Lawrence Neighbourhood would follow infill principles, though on a much larger scale.

This is one reason why we seldom speak of it as a civic achievement – and why many people who visit it, and even some who live there, remain unaware that it's a distinct entity with a unique history. The St. Lawrence Neighbourhood is pleasant, law-abiding, and mildly prosperous, and the turnover in rental apartments is encouragingly low. All of this is surprising in a government-directed area, but the neighbourhood's most unusual characteristic is also the one that hides it from us: its edges are blurred. Unlike every other government-directed scheme on the continent, it doesn't clearly indicate where it starts and stops. In the winter of 1995 I spoke with a woman who had lived since

1981 in a condominium at the southeast corner of Front and George Streets, on land that Dennis acquired for the city and then sold to a private developer. She didn't know, till I told her, that she has been living, all this time, in the St. Lawrence Neighbourhood.

Those who took Jacobs's work seriously had been talking about the need to mix tenants with varied incomes and buildings with varied uses in the same development. Public housing goes to pieces, they argued, when it is obviously separate from the surrounding city; streets turn dangerous when deprived of ordinary commerce. Littlewood started out with the idea of creating apartments and town houses that would be one third publicly owned, one third private, and one third partially subsidized; ideally, it would be impossible to tell at a glance which was which – and that's how it turned out. Stores, restaurants and even schools would be integrated into apartment buildings. Doors would face the streets, unlike the hard-to-reach entrance-ways that are standard in failed public-housing projects.

Studying successful districts like the Annex and the Beach, Littlewood and his colleagues noticed that all of them had main streets running through them. Traditional planning theory argues that traffic should be routed around residential neighbourhoods – the dead ends so common in the suburbs were laid out by planners who had absorbed this textbook aversion to ordinary roads. But the districts that work best in Toronto are not segregated enclaves, they are places people can drive through. So the St. Lawrence Neighbourhood would follow that pattern. It would also have, like most successful old districts, lanes and backyards.

To work their new buildings into the fabric of the existing city, Littlewood and his colleagues continued southward the old streets of Governor Simcoe's York. They used taller buildings, with their backs to the Gardiner and the railway tracks, as noise barriers, with triple-glazed windows and extra soundproofing. They designed The Esplanade as an east-west strip of public space, part boulevard, part park.

THERE WERE SHARP disagreements in the early days, even among politicians who were anxious to see the project go ahead. Mayor Crombie was pushing the process at a speed that some people, such as Alderman Sewell, regarded as reckless. Alderman Sewell was, in the view of Mayor Crombie, dragging his heels. A generation later, the conflict between them isn't always easy to explain. In the communal memory of Toronto, Crombie and Sewell, two famous mayors, seem to have been natural allies, because they eventually stood on the same side of so many issues. But in the 1970s they brought quite different ideas to public issues, and in everyday politics they argued more often than they agreed. Both were dedicated servants of their city, and both were conservatives in the sense that they were anxious to maintain the traditional virtues of Toronto, above all its old neighbourhoods. But while Crombie was at home in the Red Tory wing of the Progressive Conservative Party, Sewell remained outside the party system, a maverick who seemed happiest as a party of one.

Sewell entered politics almost by accident, when he was a young lawyer and was asked to do some volunteer work for a neighbourhood action committee. That experience gave him a lifelong belief in the power of organized citizen opinion, but it did not produce the knack of compromise that is essential to a political career. Sewell followed Crombie as mayor but lasted only one tumultuous term, 1978-80. Even when installed in the mayor's office, he continued to talk like an outsider, and made as many enemies as friends. Since his defeat he has been an author, a columnist for *The Globe and Mail* and for *Now* newspaper, a teacher, a royal commissioner, and a consultant. Like Crombie, he remains a much loved figure in Toronto – as recently as 1994, a *Globe* columnist suggested that he was the best possible candidate for mayor.

Crombie and Sewell were both careful and admiring students of Jane Jacobs's ideas, but they often disagreed on the way to apply them. A *Globe and Mail* clipping from November 21, 1974, conveys a whiff of the argument they were conducting in public that year. The report said Sewell had forced the executive committee of council to hold up the design study for the St. Lawrence Neighbourhood so that community groups could become more involved. Crombie, according to the *Globe,* questioned Sewell's views on public housing, noting that recently they had been in "metamorphosis." The Crombie forces were in danger, Sewell thought, of making arbitrary decisions and imposing them from above. Eventually, Crombie's plans went through, but only after satisfying Sewell's reservations.

Once started, the neighbourhood grew quickly. Most of the major buildings were in use by 1981, seven years after Lewinberg's first report, though others have been going up ever since. Various architects were used, some chosen by public agencies, some by private developers. The architects caught the spirit of the place, an odd combination of grandeur (in scale) and humility (in tone). As Littlewood says, "We didn't think of redesigning the world. We were just making a neighbourhood." Today, after some fifteen years of construction, there's not one structure in the district that looks like an expression of architectural ego. Two early buildings helped set the style: Irving Grossman's Crombie Park, which had to accommodate two schools (public and Roman Catholic) along with apartments and stores; and Jerome Markson's David B. Archer Co-op. Markson, not long after, went north of Front Street to design Market Square, an expensive condominium complex built outside the acquisition lands. Market Square fits the neighbourhood by using brick, putting stores on the street, and limiting itself to eight storeys. In the St. Lawrence style, Markson also respected the historic environment by siting his square to include a view of St. James Cathedral, a gracious twentieth-century tribute to one of the monuments of the nineteenth.

Across the neighbourhood, architects used arches and patterns of bays to create harmony with nearby Victorian buildings. Brick wasn't specified in the by-law, but one architect after another chose it, giving the district a consistent style. At that moment, the sandblasting of old brick buildings was becoming fashionable; some people, noticing these new structures for the first time, no doubt assumed they were old structures recently cleaned. As John Sewell wrote in his 1993 book, *The Shape of the City,* "St. Lawrence quickly became known as the new community downtown that felt like it had always been there – which of course was exactly what the planning committee had intended."

One of the neighbourhood's admirers is Roberta Brandes Gratz, a New York writer on urban affairs. In a 1994 book on current planning, *The Living City,* she called St. Lawrence "the best example of an appropriate large new construction project that I have found." Jane Jacobs took her there in 1977, when it was still largely derelict, and explained what was going to happen. "I listened skeptically," Gratz writes, "but then I saw it actually unfold over time in the way she predicted." She finds, as many visitors do, a few drawbacks: "a sameness to the look of it: all the buildings are of brick, with white-painted wood trim." It lacks the small, sometimes surprising changes that come when people alter their environment over time. These drawbacks are the reverse side of the neighbourhood's best qualities. As Jacobs acknowledges, it suffers aesthetically from having too much building from one historic period. Only age can give the buildings individuality and charm. St. Lawrence is not a perfect Jane Jacobs neighbourhood. Making a perfect Jane Jacobs neighbourhood takes a century or so.

On opening day, in June, 1979, Michael Dennis called St. Lawrence "a tremendous act of faith by the city in its downtown." He said, "This won't be the last downtown neighbourhood, but it could be the model for all the rest." Two years later a *Globe* article called the neighbourhood Toronto's civic laboratory community." But whatever was learned in this lab was not applied elsewhere. One promising idea, for a while, was the Ataratiri district, an old industrial area stretching east from Parliament Street to the Don River, which now has the derelict look that the St. Lawrence area had in the mid-1970s. Ataratiri would have followed the principles of the St. Lawrence Neighbourhood, on an even larger scale, but after years of study and planning it was abandoned. Pollution of the land by industry was an official reason for killing it, but the larger problem was lack of leadership. Ataratiri died because it didn't have the influential supporters and the political momentum to overcome the inevitable obstacles.

A project as ambitious as the St. Lawrence Neighbourhood requires the careful orchestration of government agencies, private developers, citizens' groups, and public opinion. Any one of those forces can defeat it. The St. Lawrence Neighbourhood came into being, above all, because talented and determined leaders – Crombie, Dennis, Sewell, and a few others– committed themselves to it, risked their reputations, and would not be stopped. The St. Lawrence Neighbourhood, at Sewell's insistence, followed democratic principles and processes, involving the public as much as possible; but process didn't make the crucial difference. As Alan Littlewood said recently, "People have too much faith in process. People think if they get the process right it will all work out, but that's wrong. You need leadership – and you need talent." You also need luck. And perhaps you need Jane Jacobs cheering from the sidelines.

6

Whose Beach?

THERE'S NOTHING LIKE an argument over names to release hidden passions. When parents and grandparents divide into warring camps over the decision to call a baby Doris or Samantha, they are asserting rival memories and conflicting claims on the future. When the Belgian Congo, having achieved independence as the Democratic Republic of the Congo, decided to change again and become Zaire, its leaders were making a statement about being African. But what can we say about a district, a fair-sized chunk of old Toronto, that does not – after seven or eight decades of existence – know its own name? The district is either the Beach, which is what most of us called it when I grew up there in the 1930s and 1940s, or the Beaches, which is what a good many of its residents call it now, over the pained objections of a good many others.

The names are much alike – but, as Mark Twain said, the difference between the right word and the nearly right word is the difference between lightning and the lightning bug. In the 1980s the issue of naming suddenly became charged with meaning, as if the very soul of the place were in question. The argument brought to the surface powerful feelings of ownership and a surprising collection of resentments, not all of them entirely coherent. We who grew up there when it was mainly lower-middle-class and distinctly unfashionable still believe that in some way we possess it, even if we moved out long ago (as I did, in 1956). Naturally, we look with disdain on those parvenus – directors of television commercials, assistant professors of marketing, disc jockeys, and the like – who discovered it around 1970. These newcomers brought fresh life to the district and prosperity to a retail strip that was dying. Old Beach people might grudgingly acknowledge that truth, but they don't dwell on it. What attracts their attention, and their passion, is the way that the post-1970 newcomers transformed it into an overheated real-estate market, Trendsville-by-the-Lake.

The Beach wasn't anything like that when I knew it best. If it is true that we learn everything important in childhood, then I learned everything important in the Beach. Some of it I learned at Williamson Road Public School, which was a place of astounding parochialism in the 1940s but now has, among other comparatively recent innovations, a French immersion unit; and at Malvern Collegiate Institute, a school of dourly limited ambition that nevertheless contained in its student body, while I was there, both the pianist Glenn Gould and a future premier of Alberta, Don Getty. Gould remained in the Beach until well into his twenties, in his parents' house at 32 Southwood Drive, where pilgrims from Japan can sometimes be seen photographing the plaque mounted in 1993 by the Toronto Historical Society.

It now seems odd that this world-conquering genius, arguably the most important instrumental performer of his age, should have spent his youth in the narrow little world of the Beach. At the time, it seemed natural and inevitable to me. In fact, everything about the Beach seemed natural and inevitable. In childhood I thought it was the way a district should be, and in adolescence I began escaping so often to downtown Toronto that the nature of the Beach no longer mattered.

And then, a few years after the 1965 opening of the New City Hall gave Toronto a public focus and a heightened self-consciousness, I became aware that something had happened to my old district. It was starting to become fashionable, and even the name was changing. Around 1969 or 1970 I began to hear people call it "the Beaches," and I associated the name with a new idea of the Beach. As an expatriate, I hated the idea of change, though many changes were clearly improvements.

I had moved far, far away – several miles away, in fact – to central Toronto. I had even made the enormous cultural leap across Yonge Street, the great historic divide of the old city, going from what was then the largely white and British half of Toronto into areas that were rich in Italians, Chinese, Ukrainians, Jews, and blacks. But the fact that I might have changed was in no sense to be taken as license for the Beach to do the same. Like all expatriates, I wanted my native land to remain as I had left it, ready for visiting at my leisure. I wanted the dowdy, sleepy little streets of my youth to remain dowdy and sleepy. I wanted Queen Street East, the grand boulevard of my Depression childhood, to remain the least fashionable shopping street in Toronto. So when I saw the changes of the 1970s, I was annoyed.

Like most old Torontonians, I didn't understand what was happening to my city and my old district, the ripples that were spreading out from Nathan Phillips Square. The Beach was becoming part of the new public urbanism that Toronto was embracing – in fact, few districts today show so clearly the transformation of Toronto from private to public. Toronto was changing from a city of mean corner restaurants to a city of cafés, from a city of silence to a city of conversation. The Beach was falling into step.

My feelings of surprise and alarm were nothing to those of the militant old Beach people still living there. For many of them, the 1970s were a cultural nightmare. It was like going to sleep in your home town and waking up in a Hollywood set. One day it was the old Beach, where the most exciting event on a summer night was the lawn bowling in Kew Gardens. The next day – or so it must have seemed – the place was a false-front simulation of alien environments. Stores that had seemed authentic and solid melted away, to be replaced by pasta restaurants, jeans shops, meticulous reproductions of English pubs, and eventually a store selling surfboards. Restaurants with names like "Nevada" appeared, and a clothing store called "Newport in the Beaches." Today, the Beach is self-consciously fashionable. Plain old Queen Street East has become a strip of restaurants offering goat's-cheese pizza and real-estate offices selling cottage-sized houses for hundreds of thousands of dollars.

NO ONE KNEW how deeply these changes were resented until 1985, the year when finally the Old Beach rose up in wrath and symbolically smote the New Beaches. That was the Year of the Signs, a year never to be forgotten in Beach history.

The crisis began as one small element in Toronto's continuing attempt to identify its districts and make them visible. The local merchants decided that commerce would be stimulated if street signs along Queen were changed to indicate the name of the neighbourhood. They were following a fashion that began in the 1970s and spread across the whole city. In the early years there were just two places officially designated by their street signs, the old Town of York and the traditional Chinatown, with signs in English and Chinese. That proved such an attractive idea that dozens of other districts acquired their own signs. Walking the streets of Toronto, you can now pick out Old Cabbagetown, Corso Italia, Bloor West Village, and many other places.

The impulse to name these sections of Toronto, some of which are otherwise undifferentiated from the neighbourhoods surrounding them, springs from two sources: the psychological need for local identity in a big city, and the desire of retailers and real-estate people to give their enterprises an aura of distinction. Not everyone finds this idea delightful. There are those who think it feels too much like the calculated charm of Disneyland. My own view is that it encourages, in at least some citizens, a sense of history and a pride in neighbourhood, qualities vital to a healthy city. But certainly it will create political problems in the future. What happens when Italians move from an Italian district, or Greeks from a Greek district – changes that are all but certain in an ethnically volatile city? Will the city take population surveys to determine when the number of residents in a given district falls below a credible level?

The problem created by signs in the Beach was more specific. One day, fourteen signs went up, declaring the district to be the Beaches. The next day, the dam of feeling burst. Outraged, the Old Beach faction went furiously to work. Many phoned their members of city council, who professed innocence; the change had never been discussed by council, they said. Others phoned their member of the Ontario legislature. Many wrote letters to editors, and to the business association that perpetrated the deed. One woman – I was delighted to see she lived on Hammersmith Avenue, where my family lived for a while in the 1940s – went door to door with a petition demanding that City Hall tear down the offending signs.

The local paper, *Ward 9 News,* received thirty-five letters, all but four of them opposed to the signs. One man wrote: "It's been sad to watch our Queen St. gradually turn into a circus for tourists.... It's even sadder to have our name bastardized from the Beach to The Beaches.... " Someone said he always called it the Beach, and "only outsiders in their ignorance refer to the Beaches." The most eloquent objector was a resident of Wineva Avenue, another street where I once lived. The signs, he said, "demean the district, just as the preponderance of eating houses and drinking parlours do." *Eating houses and drinking parlours:* the very words express another era, when it was proper to do such things in private. This gentleman said the peaceful old Queen Street he once knew had been destroyed by money. "I grieve," he wrote, "for the younger generation, their children, and their paradise lost." Later a former councilor for the area, Dorothy Thomas, said: "The Beaches is a real-estate and a commercial term. It's not a name locals use. It's a name used by outsiders." In fact, I've heard it spoken by people who grew up there, including John Sewell.

Thrown on the defensive, the business people asked plaintively that these critics "acknowledge and accept the universal law that change is inevitable." In the Beach? Never! In a few weeks of lobbying, the forces of the Beach persuaded the city to take down the signs and replace them with the simple street signs of the past. In the material, commercial world, the newcomers had won many victories, but on the ground of symbolism the old Beach was triumphant. It is unlikely that the issue will be raised again in this millennium.

IN SUMMERTIME, the Queen Street East of the late twentieth century has the feel of a tourist village. Fifty years ago, I occasionally heard people describe our district as a village, sometimes affectionately and sometimes not. Downtown Toronto was only half an hour away by streetcar, and in the Depression those of our fathers who had jobs went there to work. Otherwise, most of us stayed put, in our village.

The Beach stretches across the southeast corner of old, pre-suburban Toronto, along the lake from Greenwood Race Track (soon to be demolished) east to the Balmy Beach Canoe Club; it ends at the R. C. Harris water filtration plant on the border of Scarborough. A good deal of the history of the area resides in those three landmarks.

In 1939, when Greenwood was called Woodbine, King George VI and Queen Elizabeth attended the King's Plate, the first time the reigning monarch watched the grandest of all Canadian races; the winner that year was a horse owned by George McCullagh, the young founder of *The Globe and Mail*. The Balmy Beach Canoe Club – always notable for paddling races, lawn bowling, alcohol ingesting, and hell raising – was also notable, in the 1920s and 1930s, for its rugby team, Toronto Balmy Beach, which won the Grey Cup in 1930, becoming the first and last district team to do so (nowadays it sometimes takes a whole province to win the thing). The Harris filtration plant, planned in the 1920s and built between 1937 and 1958, is a wonderfully imaginative structure that has been praised by the architect George Baird for its "almost dreamlike imageries," which elevate a functional building into a powerful presence. In Toronto it is perhaps the most imposing example of engineering raised to art. From certain angles it appears forbidding, and often it shows up in movies and television dramas as a prison or a mental hospital – most recently, it impersonated an old-fashioned insane asylum in John Carpenter's 1995 horror film, *In The Mouth of Madness*. In 1987 it went into Canadian literary history as the setting for part of Michael Ondaatje's novel, *In the Skin of a Lion*.

North from the water, the Beach reaches up to the brow of the hill on which Kingston Road has run to the east since long before Confederation. When I was little, there were two important things about the Beach that I misunderstood, and that hill was one of them. As a child I knew that the world was round; I also knew that walking north from my house for a few blocks entailed ascending a hill. I put the two things together and deduced that the hill reflected the curvature of the earth. A teacher later explained that it was an ancient sandbar, but there are still times when the idea of the earth's roundness evokes in my mind the image of nine-year-old me walking up the steep slope of Southwood Drive toward Kingston Road.

My other misunderstanding was more typical of the ignorance of youth. I took it for granted that everyone lived in as satisfying a world as the Beach was for me. The lake, the boardwalk, and the sandy beach itself were no more than a block away. The water, in those days, was not polluted; if dead fish washed up on the shore, we assumed they had died of old age. In summer we were on the beach every day; in winter part of the lake froze over and we played dangerously on the large ice cakes along the shore, hiding in caves they had formed. The boardwalk ended at the east in a huge park and at the west in an even bigger park and the race track, the roar of its summertime crowds floating over the little houses of Woodbine Avenue. You couldn't get in until you turned sixteen, but you could watch the races from outside the fence, standing beside crowds of adults who couldn't afford the fifty-cent admission price.

Most of us were not well off, and our houses were cramped. If we lived near these vast open spaces, I assumed, then everyone did. I think I was twelve or thirteen before I learned otherwise – learned, in fact, that for a child the Beach was one of the best city places on earth and that the people living there were the lucky beneficiaries of a history they hardly knew. Early in this century, the district was founded and designed as a resort area. Since recreation was its main purpose, and land was cheap, it seemed only natural that large parcels of real estate were set aside for parks and beach. By the time city land became precious, around the middle of this century, parkland was politically untouchable.

FOR ALL THE TALK of its history, the Beach is quite new as a place to live, one of the newest places within old Toronto. Most of it was built in this century and much of it after the First World War. As late as 1865, when downtown was busy and populous, there were only a dozen houses at the Beach, and Queen Street East was a country trail littered with tree stumps. In the 1870s and 1880s, people went there to pitch a tent for a week, and a few years later they began building cottages. Steamboats and street railways reached it, but as late as the 1890s there was no streetcar service in the winter.

It was a summertime village, and hundreds of Beach houses still look like the winterized cottages they are. Because early development was erratic, you sometimes see a cottage standing beside a solidly built brick house. That also seemed natural to me as a child. Today, after zoning laws have imposed rigid standards on new communities across the continent, it looks peculiar enough to be cherished. In 1981 an architectural critic from England wrote in surprise: "There are homes in the New England style, clapboarded and shingled with wraparound verandahs, cheek-by-jowl with would-be stately mansions in formal, bow-windowed Edwardian stucco." These startling juxtapositions are sometimes made more startling because the owner of the well-made house has put a fortune into renovation and the owner of the one-time cottage has not.

At the turn of the century, the Beach was just beginning to see itself as part of the city, and Toronto was beginning to see the Beach as something more than cottage country. In 1899 a real-estate advertisement called it "the most beautiful annex of Toronto, and the coming suburban residential part of the city." In the next decade, Queen became the established commercial strip – it had sixty-five stores in 1910, more than twice that number in 1922. But the Beach still was not one continuous district. It was two residential areas, Kew Beach (to the west) and Balmy Beach (to the east). In between them was Scarboro

[sic] Beach Park, a pleasure garden modeled on Coney Island, with a tunnel of love, a shoot-the-chute, a circus, and other summertime pleasures.

While the park existed, from 1907 to 1925, the whole district was separated into three beaches, so the historical argument for "the Beaches" as a name turns out to be at least as strong as the historical argument for "the Beach." When finally the district became entirely residential, the pleasure gardens were replaced by a subdivision devoted to low-cost housing. On Wineva Avenue, one of the new streets thus created, a strip of duplexes went up. I like to think they were placed exactly on the site of the tunnel of love. My family moved into one of them in 1932, when I was a few months old. There I began my discovery of the Beach, Toronto, and the world.

THE NAMING CONTROVERSY of the 1980s indicated the peculiar quality of the Beach. It may be only a pocket of Toronto, but it sees itself as a very unusual pocket. In 1976, well after the transformation of the district began, the critic Martin Knelman wrote in *Weekend* magazine: "Even now, going to someone's house for dinner, I am struck by the fact that the Beaches [he had apparently caught the virus] has its own culture, its own sensibility, even its own politics." What Knelman picked up was the same feeling I knew as early as the 1930s – a sense of living in a big city without necessarily being a part of it.

Beach people, old or new, like to see themselves as inhabitants of a small, separate world that constantly needs to be protected from unfriendly outside forces. As early as 1907, the Beach had to fight off plans to put a railroad right through the district – plans that would have ruined the Beach waterfront in the same way that the downtown waterfront had been ruined. In the 1970s there was a serious proposal to float an offshore airport in the lake, just to the south, and another plan to cut a cross-town expressway through the district. In 1990 someone came up with a plan to mine sand from Lake Ontario, 1.5 kilometres off the Beach shoreline, raising the possibility of ecological damage. This sort of history has taught the locals to be vigilant.

Vigilance, unfortunately, sometimes turns to prejudice and bitter exclusivity. In the summer of 1933, the Beach acquired a short-lived anti-Semitic movement, the so-called swastika clubs, a protest against the appearance of outsiders on the beach. For a few weeks a number of young men actually walked the boardwalk wearing swastika badges (the Nazis had been in power for some months in Germany), but the organized opposition of Jews and the negative publicity quickly destroyed the movement. Besides, the men wearing swastikas claimed not to be anti-Semitic anyway. They insisted, with spectacular mendacity, that the swastika was just an old Indian emblem. They claimed they were merely protecting their district from outsiders, who were objectionable because they often left orange peel on the sand and immodestly changed clothes in their cars, where passersby might see them. The views of the swastika-wearers were undoubtedly bigoted, typical of the racism that often accompanies a sense of entitlement. They expressed their intolerance in a way that must have seemed natural to Torontonians of the time, masking it as a devotion to neatness and propriety.

About ten years later, when the Holocaust was raging in Europe and many young men from the Beach were fighting the Germans, some of the residents of the street where we lived perceived another threat to their way of life. Apparently a Jewish family was contemplating the purchase of a house. A petition was circulated, asking that the present owners not sell to them. Neither memory nor research can tell me what resulted (a few Jews already lived a block or two away). In any case we soon moved to another street, for unconnected reasons. I remember only two things: my parents' refusal to sign the petition, and my mother's reply when I asked her what people had against the Jews. "People say they have loud parties."

Many years later, a native of the Beach, who was about five years old in the summer of the swastika clubs, recalled the incident and defended the Beach people. "They felt," she wrote to me, "as if strangers had come and were picnicking on their front lawn." That was no excuse at all, in my view, but it fit into the Beach sensibility.

It helps explain why the transformation of Toronto in the last thirty years made some people uncomfortable. Old-time residents of the Beach do not necessarily accept the principle that public spaces are for the use of the public. They feel they own not only their houses and apartments but also the beach, the parks, even the streets. In the 1980s it became obvious that the Beach was now a recreation place for outsiders as well as locals. People came from across the Toronto region, and sometimes from farther afield, to eat, drink, shop, walk the streets, and examine this peculiar little district. They filled up the parking spaces, and in the bars late at night they were sometimes loud. The local people grew resentful, and a short-lived organization, Beach Residents Against Tourists (BRAT), sprang up. Someone printed a T-shirt that said, "Welcome to the Beach! Now go home." It was a revealing moment, a reminder that an appeal to tradition is not always an appeal to what is best in us.

7

Scarborough and Scarberia

Q: "What's the difference between Scarborough and a bus shelter?"
A: "If you really had to, you could live in a bus shelter."

THAT DIALOGUE was used in the winter of 1994 by the Komic-Kazes at the Rivoli café on Queen Street West, according to a story in the Toronto *Star.* Middle-aged readers may have wondered whether the young comedians understood that they were recycling a joke their parents told in the 1960s, but the age of the material mattered less than the power of the myth it embodied. In a peculiar way, Scarborough is central to Toronto's idea of itself. It's one of the folkloric traditions of the city, and it provides a rich playground for anyone seeking to understand the movement of impulses and opinions in society. The legendary Scarborough may have little to do with contemporary reality, but describing the truth of life in Scarborough never weakens the myth.

In Scarborough, salmon and trout spawn, under the wary eyes of white-tailed deer stopping to drink from the Rouge River. In the northwest corner of Scarborough, wealthy immigrants from Hong Kong dine at magnificent oriental restaurants, and explain that they find the cuisine in the old downtown Chinatown around Spadina Avenue unsophisticated. In the 1980s a priest in southern Scarborough told me that his big problem was keeping the anti-Communist Nicaraguan refugees who were sometimes lodged in his church basement from fighting with the pro-Communist Guatemalan refugees who shared the space. In the northeast corner of Scarborough there are Mennonite farms, and one of the few untouched Seneca burial grounds anywhere....

No one will believe any of this, of course. Everybody outside Scarborough knows that it contains nothing but strawberry-box bungalows inhabited by Canadian-born whites with British or Irish names who decorate their living rooms with paintings on velvet bought from the backs of trucks. This legendary Scarborough is so embedded in the Toronto imagination that it's believed even by some Scarborough people. In downtown Toronto it's passed on as gospel from generation to generation.

One morning in the 1980s students from a midtown Toronto school visited a Scarborough courtroom on a field trip. As their bus crossed the municipal border one of the girls cried, "Help! I feel a desperate urge to wear polyester!" For the rest of the trip the students happily topped each other's Scarborough jokes. These were liberal and liberated students, from a free experimental school, and no word of racial or religious bigotry could ever be spoken in their presence. But they knew that Scarborough jokes were not only acceptable, they were proof of sophistication. Certainly those kids would have been mortified if someone had called them snobs.

"What is this about Scarborough?" a film editor from England once asked me. We were in a house in the Annex and someone had just said something nasty about Scarborough. In a three-week visit to Toronto, the man from England told me, he had been gratuitously informed half a dozen times that Scarborough was a miserable place. I tried to explain that in the collective imagination of Metropolitan Toronto, Scarborough plays the role hell plays in Christianity – it stands for what we fear, the future we're desperate to avoid. The journalist Barbara Moon, who has lived near the Scarborough Bluffs for many years, once wrote that Scarborough is essential to the self-image of Toronto. "A Torontonian would rather be dead than redneck," she said. "But to be savoured, his superior urbanity requires a contrast, a wrongheaded, boring, inferior and faintly ridiculous collectivity...that can stand for all he disavows. This is Scarborough's special, crucial function."

Howard Engel, the detective-story writer, put it another way: "Scarborough is what we have instead of Jersey City." It's our anti-city, the dark side of the gleaming urban paradise that Torontonians sometimes imagine – in their giddiest moments of world-class smugness – they have created. In 1969 Engel notably broadened Scarborough mythology when he wrote, for CBC Radio, a parody of "A Child's Christmas in Wales," by Dylan Thomas. "A Child's Christmas in Scarborough" began:

"Whenever I remember Christmas as a child in Scarborough, I can never remember whether the slush was new or old, or whether we lived on the sixth street north of the shopping plaza stoplights and I was seven years old, or whether it was the seventh street and I was six.... "

That turned out to be something of a classic, heard on the CBC every Christmas for decades. In 1969 Engel had seldom even visited Scarborough. Why choose it for his setting? "It was the opposite of Swansea in Dylan Thomas's piece," he recalled recently. "It was that flat, amorphous place that nothing exciting could ever happen in." But the Toronto region abounds in flat, amorphous places where, at least in theory, nothing exciting could happen. Why did all this get attached to Scarborough? And why can't Scarborough shake it?

Over the last ten years, an artist of another kind, the painter Glenn Priestley, has approached Scarborough in a different spirit. Priestley is an imaginative realist whose paintings are shown at the Mira Godard Gallery in Toronto and the Wunderlich Gallery in New York. He is to Scarborough what Canaletto is to Venice: a native son who celebrates the charms of the place where he grew up. A typical Priestley painting, *Spring,* poetically depicts pale light bouncing off a parking lot, a drainage ditch, and a hydro pole. Going about his work, he arouses the curiosity of strangers: people can't imagine why he does what he does. His explanation ("Through history artists have painted their surroundings, so why should I be any different?") doesn't satisfy those born to the knowledge that Scarborough is nowhere. Once, when he was sketching a row of tract houses, a woman stopped and asked him, "Why don't you paint something that looks nice?" She had lived on that street for twenty years, she thought it looked terrible, and she held the firm opinion that appropriate artistic subjects are to be found elsewhere.

The critic Robert Stacey, in the catalogue of a Priestley exhibition at the University of Waterloo in 1989, explained the painter's project: "To describe . . . without irony, condescension or sarcasm, the kind of background shared, after all, by the majority of North Americans." Priestley may be the first artist who has caught the delicate poetry of twilight falling on a row of identical subdivision houses, and he makes autumn in Scarborough look as enchanting as autumn in Algonquin Park. But the reaction to his work – always admiring, often puzzled – illustrates the power of the Scarborough myth.

Tell people from elsewhere about some surprising aspect of the place – for instance, the Dragon Centre mall, where not only the storekeepers and the customers but even the illuminated signs are Chinese – and they'll tell you "that isn't really Scarborough." Scarborough may have the best zoo in the country and the television studio that produces programs for the CTV network, but those aren't the real Scarborough either. Nor, for that matter, is the powerful building by John Andrews that houses Scarborough College, the eastern campus of the University of Toronto, or the outdoor Greek stage at the Guild Inn, designed by Ron Thom from Neo-Classical remnants left behind when the Bank of Toronto at King and Bay Streets was torn down in 1966; it's the focus of the most eccentric sculpture park in the country, an elephant's burial ground of taste, where visitors wander in a post-modern daze among the Corinthian columns of ancient Toronto buildings.

Whatever isn't Scarberia, isn't Scarborough. You can find this form of denial even in people who have spent many years there. An eminent television producer lived in Agincourt, a section of

Scarborough, in the 1960s. He paid Scarborough taxes and voted for the Scarborough council and school board. "But," he said later, "I never felt we were living in *Scarborough*." A book publisher purchased a lovely little house near the lake, in what she thought was the Beach district, where she had always wanted to live. When she received the legal papers she discovered to her horror that the house was across the municipal boundary, just east of Neville Park Boulevard. Unknowingly, she had condemned herself to live in Scarborough!

If you talk to people living there you find, not unreasonably, a certain defensiveness. Rev. Harold Roberts, rector at St. Timothy's Anglican Church in Agincourt, began to understand the human complexity of Scarborough not long after he arrived. His congregation included, as he said, "black, Chinese, you name it," but people elsewhere imagined he was living in a white-bread nightmare. "I come from North Toronto. When my brother heard I was being transferred to this parish, he sent me a card with skyline which was totally flat except for a single bump representing a high-rise. It was supposed to be Scarborough. It's as if people think: if you're not living in Toronto, you're not in." Joanne Kates, the restaurant critic of *The Globe and Mail,* once wrote: "I am mystified by the suburbs, and more so by the people who choose to live in them." She was in the process of trashing a Szechuan restaurant at Scarborough Town Centre.

THE REASONS for all this can be found in geography, architecture, history, and – an uncomfortable word Toronto people hate to utter – class. Geographically, Scarborough started out in the wrong place. In the railroad age, the east side of everywhere was thought to be a bad address. Across North America, winds from the west routinely drove the soot eastward and left air in the western suburbs relatively pure. As Toronto grew, it followed the common pattern, and it seemed natural to put the poorer suburbs east of the old city. This eventually produced an ironic result. Nowadays it would be hard to say that one suburb's air is better than another's, but there's no question which side of the city is tougher for automobile commuters. If you live in one of the western suburbs, like Oakville, you drive straight into the sun in the morning and again at the end of the day. By comparison, Scarborough is an easy commute.

The name goes back to 1793, when Elizabeth Simcoe, the wife of the governor, noticed that the gray cliffs facing the lake looked like those of Scarborough in England. The Scarborough of today began to take shape just after the Second World War, when returning servicemen were anxious for homes and the federal government was ready to lend them down payments. There were then about 25,000 people scattered across the township, some of them on farms and more of them spread along Kingston Road. In those days, local geography was described by bus-stop numbers – as in, "I live three houses east of Stop 14."

This was the Scarborough I knew as I grew up in the Beach. It was a nearby wilderness. With other boys I'd bike along Kingston Road and "camp" – that is, cook an eggs-and-bacon lunch over an open fire – beside Highland Creek. Every spring, Grade 8 students from our public school went on a picnic to a place in Scarborough called the Willows, which had a swimming hole and "a dance hall" with a jukebox. In 1947 it also had a sign that said gentiles only, possibly the last such sign in what is now Metropolitan Toronto.

In those days Scarborough people were mostly British in origin, and mostly Protestant. In 1948 they elected as reeve a former Baptist minister, Oliver Crockford, who stayed in the job for seven years and more or less created modern Scarborough. He was a "populist," in the peculiar Toronto meaning of the word: a politician who simultaneously represents the working class *and* the land developers. Crockford was willing to issue building permits for more houses, of smaller size, than any other reeve. This allowed the developers (to quote a *Globe* editorial of the day) "to crowd the largest possible number of houses on each acre, and move on, leaving the municipality to stew in the problems thus created.... The lack of zoning will make large sections virtual slums within a very short time."

Mr. Scarborough, as Crockford liked to be called, claimed that he, and only he, was providing houses the workers could buy. The workers weren't always grateful, particularly when they realized that the sewers, roads, and schools Scarborough could offer in the early days were sometimes pitiful. Crockford built first and thought later, if at all. Nor was public transport a great interest of his. His Scarborough was a place where everyone was expected to own a car. Fittingly, he was retired by the voters on an issue of personal transportation: a judicial inquiry found that the Cadillac he was fond of driving around the township had been purchased from a developer for so low a price that the word "bribe" was hard to avoid.

Other municipalities later followed Crockford-like planning principles, but he was first with the most. His recklessness laid the foundation of Scarborough's grim reputation. But did he create slums? As it turned out, the *Globe* was wrong: the real slum creators in Toronto turned out to be careless bureaucrats who built public housing projects. Some houses of the Crockford era have been torn down, and others look as if they should be, but the slums never materialized. David Lewis Stein of the *Star*, who holds a degree in urban planning, looks on the streets laid out by Crockford as a touching monument to their era and its ideals: "This was the dream. When people came back from the Second World War they wanted to be part of this new suburban world where everything was fresh and clean. Forty-some years later, the houses have individual characteristics – go down some of those streets and you'll see that people have a genius for making things their own, making them unique. Looking at them, you can hardly imagine that they were all built at the same time by the same person, from the same cookie-cutter pattern."

Crockford gave Scarborough the closest thing to a class identity that any municipality in the Toronto region ever acquired. Few Canadians make regular use of the term "working class," but that, in effect, became the character of early Scarborough. Today Scarborough ranks fourth in average family income among the six sections of Metropolitan Toronto; it has more than its share of stenographers and security guards, less than its share of doctors and lawyers. It has, proportionately, the most public housing units. When middle-class people elsewhere express disdain for Scarborough they are expressing disdain for the class slightly beneath them.

Crockford departed in 1955. In the next decade or so, Scarborough still meant endless rows of bungalows, stretching to the horizon, interrupted now and then by a school or a mall. In the late 1960s, when the population was reaching 300,000 – about six times what it had been in 1950 – the municipal government began to address the problem of identity. In downtown Toronto, Viljo Revell's New City Hall had demonstrated how architecture could produce a sense of public purpose and bring a district to life. In 1968, the architect Raymond Moriyama was asked to lay out a city centre that would, as Scarborough council's chief planner said, "provide a focus and identity for the people of Scarborough."

There was a large piece of farmland in roughly the geographic centre. It was thought that a city hall might go there, along with a "downtown." Years later, discussing the problems of suburbs, Moriyama quoted Gertrude Stein's famous remark about Oakland: "When you get there, there's no there there." Moriyama decided to put an emphatic *there* in the middle of Scarborough. He designed a city hall that was isolated in a large open square, monumental on the outside but intimate and informal on the inside – the offices are open to the public and look into a courtyard with a carp pool and trees. The people who work there seem to like it, and crowds show up to hear free concerts on Sundays and skate on the outdoor rink. But no one would deny that from the outside it's forbidding: unlike Revell, Moriyama failed to solve the problem of making a building at once grand and inviting. He provided plenty of open space, but it was undefined and alienating. Jane Jacobs once called the building "the worst thing I've ever seen in Metro...vainglorious and inhuman."

It opened in 1973, and so did the large mall across the square. The creation of a city core was apparently under way, but as the years passed it failed to take form. "One tries to be patient,"

Moriyama has said, "but it was a long time coming." The Civic Centre opening coincided with the first oil shock, which raised gas prices and made reachable-by-subway places in downtown Toronto even more attractive than before. Another problem, perhaps, was that much of the surrounding land was owned by the Eaton's department-store empire, whose approach to development tended toward caution. In any case, years passed before the growth of Scarborough's city core picked up. Eventually Bell Canada and the federal government put in buildings. In 1985 the large Consilium office centre opened, and an elevated rapid-transit line from the Kennedy subway station finally reached the city centre. But as a business district, downtown Scarborough remains incomplete, a kind of rough sketch for something that might develop later.

EVER SINCE CROCKFORD, Scarborough politicians and boosters have been notable for the silliness of their public remarks. Gus Harris said in an article published in 1988, the year he retired as mayor, that the city core was now so close to perfection that "once a cultural centre has been built, there will be no need to go to downtown Toronto." The politicians sound even sillier when they insist that Scarborough be called by its legally correct term, a "city," though everyone knows it's no such thing. They reach their silliest when they deal with "Scarberia."

That word appeared, so far as anyone can tell, in the 1960s – at the point when Toronto was becoming self-conscious about urbanism. It was, ironically, the moment when Scarborough was beginning to shed many of the characteristics of a standard suburb. But it caught on, and for years you could hear it across Metropolitan Toronto. In my experience it ceased to be common some years ago – except among Scarborough politicians and developers. They keep going back to it, like a tongue to a tooth cavity; they raise it to deny that it now applies.

In February, 1985, for example, a member of Scarborough council publicly objected to a greeting card that satirized the bleakness of Scarborough – her city, she said, "is no longer a Scarberia." Her views were seconded later that year by the man who developed the Consilium: his complex, he said, "is the death of Scarberia – it's gone. We killed it with this project." Well, not quite. In May, 1988, when Controller Joyce Trimmer announced her campaign for the mayor's job, she said, "The city of Scarborough needs strong leadership if it is to shed its 'Scarberia' image." Two months later, Mayor Gus Harris said in an interview, "They won't be calling this place Scarberia for much longer."

This municipal masochism is also a form of defensiveness, like the habit some people have of mentioning their visible flaws – baldness, say, or obesity – before others can point them out. When I visited Mayor Trimmer's office a few years ago, she introduced the term precisely three minutes after our interview began. "I'm sick and tired of having Scarberia thrown at us, because, in fact, Scarborough is really quite a nice place to live." Well, *I* hadn't mentioned it.

The Scarborough she served in the late 1980s and 1990s had nothing much in common with the Scarborough of legend. By then about half the housing units were apartments, multiples, or townhouses, and far more apartments and condominium buildings than houses were being planned. Ethnically, Scarborough is now about as mixed as any part of the Toronto area. But Mayor Trimmer believed that a great deal depended on reshaping its image. When she became mayor she put that question at the top of her agenda, and not only for reasons of local pride. She imagined that Scarborough's future might be shaped by what the rest of us think about it.

The people living in Scarborough make many of the decisions about their future, but their community is also affected by politicians and civil servants in the provincial and Metropolitan Toronto governments. Such people could decide, for instance, whether to put a gigantic garbage dump there, or run an expressway through. If they believe they're dealing with Scarberia, which is already pretty horrible, then why should they worry about destroying its environment? Who cares about ripping the fabric of a community that doesn't, apparently, exist? Certainly we can't expect decision-makers to think about white-tailed deer of whose existence they are ignorant.

Humans are pattern-making animals. We need to organize and classify knowledge just to be able to think about it. But this necessary impulse also produces rigid prejudice. What begins as useful classification can easily turn into glib untruth. It may be, for instance, that the word "yuppie" once carried the seed of an insight, but in the 1980s it quickly became a way of dismissing people we didn't like by freezing them in a category. "Ethnic" is a perfectly good word, but categorizing non-British, non-French Canadians as "ethnics" is one of the abominations of recent Canadian politics; it's a way of expressing superiority while assembling people into groups for the purpose of political exploitation. In Toronto, Scarborough provides the best example of how prejudice outweighs experience and an artificial construct becomes more potent than reality.

Previous page: Where the new Toronto was born: Viljo Revell's 1965 New City Hall and Nathan Phillips Square, a romantic departure from modernist geometry and a stage to act out the life of a city.

Above: A residence on the Island, the embattled community in Toronto Harbour, focus of political controversy for four decades. Was Toronto large-spirited enough to tolerate such an odd little collection of mostly odd little houses?

Above left: Hundreds of ravines, winding through the city, give Toronto its unique topographical identity as a gigantic park that happens to contain a city, "San Francisco turned upside down."

Above: The biggest piece of urban furniture in the city, the Frederick G. Gardiner Expressway, a monument to the most powerful politician in Toronto history – one generation's dream, another generation's nightmare.

Left: Frank Darling's rococo Bank of Montreal at the northwest corner of Front and Yonge Streets – an exuberantly triumphant design in 1885, reduced to doll-house scale by modern towers, now part of the Hockey Hall of Fame.

Above: A Georgian survivor from the colonial period, The Grange, built in 1817–18 by the Boulton family, the first of many architectural events on land granted by the Crown as Park Lot Thirteen.

Right: The noblest space in the 1993 version of the Art Gallery of Ontario, the Tanenbaum Atrium, an anthology of architectural history attached to the north wall of The Grange.

Overleaf: One of the happiest downtown surprises of the 1990s, Baird and Sampson's poetic Piranesi-inspired Bay-Adelaide Park, the only finished section of a mega-development that was stopped in its tracks when the real-estate boom died.

8

Islanders

PERHAPS IT DIDN'T actually change anything. Perhaps the community would have been saved anyway. But in the mythology of the Island – that most romantic slice of Toronto, that embattled sandbar bohemia in the bay – the Day of the Bridge, July 28, 1980, was the most marvelous of days, the day when Islanders all stood firm in the rain and saved their homes and their souls, saved them from the bulldozers and the barbarians in the Metro parks department. Islanders remember where they were that day, as others remember where they were when they heard that John Kennedy had been shot.

In recent years the Day of the Bridge has come up often in conversation, as a relief from the emotional strain of the Islanders' struggle to define themselves in the new world created by the Ontario government – a world that for the first time wants them to stay where they are, govern themselves, and even increase in number. They are a community of natural anarchists trying to become solid citizens, and this has turned out to be more painful than they expected. The Day of the Bridge evokes a happier time, when they feared for the future but agreed on the most important fact in politics, the identity of the enemy.

In 1980 they had been under siege for more than two decades, a community heading toward all but certain extinction. The Metro parks department owned the Island – actually, an archipelago of eighteen variously sized islands, but always called "the

Island." Metro had already demolished most of the old houses and wanted the last Islanders to leave so that the houses on Ward's Island and Algonquin Island, the two remaining communities, could be torn down to make the large Island Park even larger. Metro had the law on its side. The Islanders had their intense feeling of community and their hatred of big government and its autocratic ways.

Their chief enemy for many years was Tommy Thompson, the Metro parks commissioner. Elsewhere he was known as a lovable servant of the people who led folksy nature walks on the weekend and dotted his empire of greenery with friendly signs saying "Please walk on the grass." On the Island, however, his reputation was little better than Hitler's – in a 1973 Toronto *Star* column, the late Alexander Ross, an Islander for years, borrowed the Nazi phrase "Final Solution" to describe Thompson's vision of an unpeopled Island. Thompson gave a Toronto *Sun* reporter his view of the Islanders' "emotional, sentimental case" in 1976: "They said to hell with leases, to hell with the law. I have been spoken of in very bad terms over there and I don't think I have done anything except carry out what I was asked to do." Metro had decided that just about all of the Island should become recreation space, and he had merely followed Metro's wishes. Besides, he thought from the beginning that the houses, many of them originally built as summer cottages, were of little value and deserved destruction.

Thompson retired in 1978 (he died in 1985) but the fight with Metro went on, and the Islanders kept losing. They lost all the way to the Supreme Court of Canada, which upheld Metro's legal right to take possession of the houses. That looked like the end of the story. By the summer of 1980 the Islanders had nothing on their side but Toronto city council, which had responded to a generation of feverish lobbying, and the vague feeling among many mainlanders that the Island community was worth saving. The issue had become a kind of test: many Torontonians with no connection to the Island wanted to save it both for its own value and for the sake of the city's soul. Was Toronto generous and large-spirited enough to tolerate and encourage such an odd little collection of mostly odd little houses? Or would the drive toward a rationalized, organized city prove stronger than our ability to tolerate variety?

In those terms it was a moral as well as a political issue. The Islanders, of course, believed profoundly in the justice of their cause. In *The Robber Bride,* Margaret Atwood catches their mood through Charis, a New Age mystic who lives on the Island: "The city wants to tear down all these houses... Charis sees it as envy: if the city people can't live here themselves they don't want anyone else to be able to do it either." On July 1, 1980, Dominion Day, the Islanders held a public rally, and Jane Jacobs came over from the Annex to make a passionate statement against the plans of the Metro parks department: "This community shouldn't be destroyed. It shouldn't be destroyed because it's lovable. It's unique. It's wicked to destroy lovable, unique and lovely things."

The Islanders knew the sheriff would arrive soon with eviction notices, and they decided to stop him by civil disobedience. They put a war-surplus siren on the roof of a clubhouse to warn of his coming, and they equipped themselves with walkie-talkies and yellow hard hats labeled HOME GUARD. They had a secret sympathizer in the sheriff's office, and on a drizzly Monday morning their mole called to say the sheriff would soon be on his way. The siren began to wail, just after most of the Islanders had left on the ferry for their jobs in the city. Phone calls brought them hurrying home. The Island Navy, a fleet of water taxis and small boats, was sent out to get them (along with friendly reporters and television crews), in case Metro parks tried to frustrate the demonstration by stopping the ferry service. "It was like a reverse Dunkirk," one of the Islanders fondly remembers.

Rick/Simon (an artist who insists on the diagonal stroke) put on his hard hat and helped chain some picnic tables to trees, closing off one route the sheriff's cars might take. The Islanders wanted to stage the confrontation at the place of their choosing, by the bridge where the road leads to both Algonquin and Ward's. Rick/Simon was one of twenty members of the Flying Toad Squad, the elite shock troops who planned to lock arms around any house the sheriff approached, and go to jail if necessary. He still has a proud memento of that period imbedded in the wall of his house on Lakeshore Avenue: a big industrial hook, to which he planned to chain himself as a last-ditch protest when the bulldozers arrived.

Soon they were all at the bridge, the people from the city and the retired people and the children, released from the Island school to swell the crowd. A banner appealing to the premier of Ontario stretched across the road: SAVE US BILL DAVIS. They waited for hours, rain dripping off their ponchos. In mid-afternoon the sheriff arrived from Centre Island in a police car (there are no private cars on the Island, just the vehicles of police, firefighters, and the parks department). When he came into view, the Islanders sang, "Like a tree standing by the water, we shall not be moved." And then, just as in the dreams many of them had nourished since their hippie years, non-violent protest actually worked. They were not moved. Leaders of the community talked to the sheriff, asking for a delay. Confronted by a mob large enough to be intimidating, he agreed. Notices were not served. Later Sally Gibson wrote in her book, *More Than An Island*: "As the officials retreated, to the wild cheers of Islanders and their friends, the sun came out."

AT THAT POINT the Islanders could count on the support, more or less, of Toronto city council, and the undying enmity of the Metro government. Ontario was apparently neutral, but six months later it began moving over to the side of the Islanders, nudged by Larry Grossman, an influential cabinet minister whose constituency stretched to the Island. A report commissioned by the Ontario government recommended that the houses still standing be left in place for twenty-five years, and the legislature embodied that idea in law. Metro refused to admit defeat, and one Metro chairman later went so far as to call the Islanders "terrorists," but the community acquired some security. Even so, it was still scheduled to die eventually, and the city couldn't issue building permits to expand or improve the houses. Whatever construction was done (and there was a good deal) happened illegally.

The election of the Ontario New Democratic Party government in 1990 changed everything. The department of municipal affairs commissioned another report, this one from Richard Johnston, a former NDP member of the legislature and a supporter of the Island cause. Johnston said that the Island communities should become permanent, and even grow. He argued that the 650 or so people living there weren't enough to make a working community (the Island hasn't supported even a convenience store in many years) and the public school can be justified only if it attracts more pupils. Johnston proposed constructing 100 or so new houses, raising the population to about 900.

But who would own the Island houses, and the land beneath them? Johnston proposed that the residents own their houses and sign ninety-nine-year leases for the land, which would remain public. Islanders would be able to leave both houses and leases to their descendants, but they would never be allowed to profit by selling them. Like most politicians who have studied the dispute, Johnston understood that windfall profits going to Islanders, after all those years of bitter controversy, would be unpalatable to taxpayers elsewhere. He proposed that a new level of government – eventually called the Toronto Islands Residential Community Trust Corporation – manage the land, under a board mainly elected and partly appointed by the government. Islanders would take out leases with the trust, and if they decided to move away they would sell them back to the trust at a fair price – they would have, in Johnston's term, "curtailed ownership." The trust would support itself, levying taxes if necessary, and would manage the construction of new housing.

In 1992 the Ontario legislature turned Johnston's ideas into law. People on Ward's Island pay $36,000 for their ninety-nine-year leases, those on Algonquin (where the lots are bigger) $46,000. The money repays the city's investment in the Island. The province acquired the land through a swap, giving Metro in return the Lakeshore psychiatric hospital property. The deal had something for everyone: the city got some money, Metro got a new location for a park, the Islanders got security, and the Ontario government got a rare political victory – at no financial cost. After all those years of struggle, the Island community became a permanent part of the Toronto cityscape. And the Islanders, having achieved just about everything they ever wanted – well, they must have been in heaven, right?

NOT EXACTLY. Government played on the Islanders the same dirty trick that the Soviet Union played on the West by collapsing – or so, at least, it appeared to this visitor (I owned a summer cottage on Ward's for a few years in the 1960s, but am otherwise a mainlander). The events of the 1990s robbed the Islanders of their common enemy, and set them to fighting among themselves. Island politics turned sour, which means more than it might in other places. The battle for survival had made politics everyone's daily bread, and Islanders had produced more political controversy per capita than any other Canadians. Now they were fated to live under more governments than anyone else – Ottawa, Ontario, the Municipality of Metropolitan Toronto, the City of Toronto, and their new midget municipality, the community trust. "There is more government in Canada than any other place in the world," says a Newfoundlander in *The Shipping News,* a much-admired novel by the American writer E. Annie Proulx. By that measure, the Toronto Islanders are now the ultimate Canadians.

Inventing this latest government was far more difficult than anyone imagined. In November, 1993, the Islanders held an election to choose ten representatives to serve on an interim board to organize the trust. It seemed a simple matter, but on the Island nothing political is simple and this event became so contentious that people were still talking about it, months later, in angry tones. After the election, the pages of the Toronto Island Residents' Association Newsletter filled up with complaints about sleazy political tactics, dirty tricks, a ruling elite, ideological conflict, and fear mongering. Someone even expressed a pious wish that Islanders could "avoid the civil strife seen in newly independent nations around the world." Anyone reading these ferociously polemical comments would find it hard to remember that only 336 votes were cast in the election, and that the board members were to serve, unpaid, for only six months.

What had caused the trouble? On the surface it was a matter of slates. Someone drew up a slate of candidates who were committed to developing the trust as the Ontario government intended; some people regarded that ordinary political practice as offensively elitist. Another slate appeared, with different candidates. The slates were not universally distributed, and some of those whose names appeared on them claimed they never saw one. Six months later this was still a subject of nervous conversation and timorous self-censorship. When asked who had drawn the slates, some elected members of the board said they knew but were not going to "name names," as one put it – as if a crime had been committed. Somehow, the idea that a slate was inherently sleazy entered the bloodstream of the Islanders, and even the earnest, dedicated chair of the interim trust, Doryne Peace, had to acknowledge that "this unhappy first election" left a legacy of mistrust.

Beneath the talk about ideologies and slates there was an issue of some substance: ownership. The Islanders live in a park, and the land was already owned by the public in 1858, when a storm drove a hole in the mainland (where the Eastern Gap is now) and created the Island. Nevertheless, there are Islanders who still dream of being property owners. Why can't they treat their houses as their principal investments, the way millions of other Canadians do? Why can't they hope to do as owners in Cabbagetown did when that downtown district suddenly became fashionable in the 1970s, and what were once slum properties sold for huge profits? Some Islanders dreamt of that happening to them.

It's possible to imagine such a result, but only in another place, with a different history. The Conservative provincial government elected in June, 1995, is sympathetic to private ownership, but if it applies that ideology to the Island it will charge far higher land rents, or sell the land at high prices. That could push out many Islanders, about a fifth of whom have household incomes under $20,000. An ownership system would also confirm every hostile word ever uttered or published about the selfishness of people insisting they be allowed to live on parkland. Finally, it would destroy precisely the sense of community that had been the Islanders' central argument for thirty years.

Only a small minority have voiced such an idea, even in private, but it became the subtext of many political discussions, seldom spoken but never entirely forgotten. It may have helped create the nightmarishly populist approach to decision-making that took hold among the Islanders, an approach that seemed to prove that even democracy can be carried to a pathological level. The Islanders decided they wanted to vote en masse, at public meetings, for all sorts of things that are decided everywhere else by elected politicians – site planning, budgets, leases, by-laws, and of course taxes. Worse, they wanted to vote by secret ballot. In the old days Islanders voted by show of hands, but early in 1994 they arrived at the idea that it's best to keep voting secret, no matter how trivial the issue. This made it impossible to amend whatever was put before a meeting; the community, when gathered together, didn't generate ideas or solutions, just decisions – and not too many of those. On one Sunday afternoon about seventy people went to a public meeting at the Algonquin Island Association clubhouse. Their purpose was to decide how to manage the vote on a budget issue. There were five methods of voting to consider, and their task was to select one. They spent three hours, and at the end they had instead expanded the list of options to seventeen.

The intimacy of Island life charged all this democracy with exceptional emotion. Islanders see themselves as hardy nonconformists, and outsiders tend to endorse that idea. Chris Wilson, a mainlander hired to run the community trust, has said, "Islanders are independent, strong-minded, not easily stampeded." He sees those as characteristics of people who choose to live on an island with limited access. All true, but there's also a closeness not everyone can handle. A few hundred people share not only a small piece of land but also the daily ferry rides to and from the city. At times they are more like a huge family than a small village, and they can develop a paranoid obsession with family secrets. Rick/Simon, who was elected to the interim board, tried to explain why the secret ballot became necessary:

"People do not want their neighbours to know where they stand on things. Because their neighbours may want to excommunicate them if they come out on the wrong side. It's horrendous." On a beautiful June Sunday, when I arrived at the Ward's Island boat dock, I ran into an old acquaintance, a longtime Islander, and told her I had noticed that conflicts were arising within the community. "Yes," she said. "Now it's the enemies within." No wonder they liked talking about the Day of the Bridge.

THE ISLANDERS ARE sorting out their internal politics, as they have sorted out other issues in the past, but the long process raised a question: Is the Island worth all the trouble? For those who cherish the idea of Toronto as a city of infinite variety, the answer is an emphatic *yes.* In the old, pre-1956 days, before Metro decided to replace troublesome human beings with antiseptic parks, the Island occupied a special place in the civic imagination, somewhere between summer resort and artists' colony. It was a separate world, yet only twelve minutes across the bay by ferry. It was always cheap but never a slum, a raffish little place that grew more lovable as Toronto itself grew bigger. In the early 1950s the Main Drag at Centre Island, with its cheap hotels, rooming houses, and dance halls, was like nothing else in Toronto. It had its own glamour, particularly in the Victorian summer houses on the lakefront, with their rococo wooden fronts. Alas, those houses were among the first to be destroyed by the parks department. The rest of the Island houses were humbler, many of them winterized cottages, many others hurriedly built. But the Island retained an exotic quality, heightened by its location, at once nearby and isolated.

In 1955 Hans Blumenfeld, the assistant director of the Metro Planning Department, recommended that any plan for the Island should include both parks and people: "Without the residences, the Island would be a less interesting place." Metro's decision to ignore Blumenfeld's advice was a tragedy, as many urban-minded politicians (including David Crombie and John Sewell) have argued. Even today, with their number reduced by about two thirds (in the old days 2,000 people lived there all year), the residents remain a kind of a tourist attraction. They give the huge park a sense of life it otherwise lacks.

But is all the effort worthwhile for the Islanders themselves? Aside from struggling with government, they must struggle much harder than most of us just to buy groceries or get a plumber or someone to fix the gas. There's a water taxi, but a short trip costs twenty-four dollars. The ferry boat schedule governs everyone's existence, and the details of ordinary life require far more planning than on the mainland. Loblaws delivers food once a week, a milkman comes on Monday and Thursday.

And not everyone finds the community a wonderful place. Teenagers often loathe it. As children they roam free through a kind of paradise, without automobiles or most of the other city dangers, exploring their natural universe. At puberty, however, their opinion of their surroundings radically changes. There's nowhere to hang out, high schools are all on the mainland, and the ferry boats impose an unforgiving curfew – the last boat leaves the city dock at 11:15 P.M., an insultingly early hour to a sixteen-year-old. Teenagers also dislike the Island for much the same reason adults love it, the intense community life. Everyone knows everything about everyone, which can be a major nuisance to those moving shakily toward adult sexual identity. Even so, when they pass through adolescence many Island-raised people return, often to the same houses they grew up in.

In the winter of 1993, when political tension was reaching new levels, the worst weather since the 1970s severely tested the faith of even the most determined Islanders. The bay froze over for two and a half months, which meant that the ferry stopped running. A few brave or foolish Islanders sometimes walked the few hundred yards across the ice, and a few others were glad of the chance to use their ice boats. Most, though, had to take a bus from their communities at the eastern end of the Island to the place on the west end where a ferry crosses the tiny gap between the Island airport and the city. Waiting for the bus in the subarctic wind was often painful, and usually the bus was overcrowded, loaded with bundle buggies the Islanders use to bring home everything from hardware to liquor. The morning trip across the Island could take half an hour, and after getting to the mainland people had to walk a good distance through the wind to public transit. There must have been times when many of them wondered why they were enduring all this.

Fred Gaysek, who has been active in Island politics for years, apparently never wondered. In some ways he's a typical Islander, a Queen Street West artist and commercial musician. He learned about the Island through artists who lived there, came as a tenant in 1982, and purchased a place on Ward's in 1984. He noticed, among the Islanders, a generous spirit, a love of spontaneous celebrations combined with a sense of responsibility for the place they lived. "I really enjoyed that combination of play and community vision. I very quickly felt I had found a home." Today he loves taking visitors around the Island and showing them its peculiar qualities as a community – the way people share their gardens, for instance. On Ward's Island, if you slip through the space between a couple of houses, you may find a communal garden, used by several families. These Islanders have created a miniaturized version of the English residential square that began appearing in the eighteenth century.

Gaysek isn't concerned that his house, facing onto the big open space beside the Ward's ferry dock, attracts the curiosity of strangers; he loves coming home and finding that a watercolour painter has set up her easel in front of his home. He's the sort of public-spirited citizen who willingly pays the price of these pleasures. As a member of many committees, he acknowledges that developing Island democracy has been troublesome, but he doesn't doubt that the Island deserves all the effort he and his friends put into it.

Even in winter? "It's wonderful in the winter." On a bright Saturday morning, when the lagoons are frozen over, he puts on his skates and joins a kind of an open-air party that reaches into every corner of the lagoon system. "I'll skate as long as I can – on Saturday I might go out at noon and not come back till sunset. You can spend the whole day constantly running into other Islanders. Old people, young people, mothers pushing children in strollers, people offering each other drinks from their flasks." Sometimes he skates across the bay to the city.

What the Island proves, better than most Toronto districts, is that not all lives in a big city need to conform to a few familiar patterns. Difference is everything to the Islanders; there's even a difference between the two communities, Ward's and Algonquin. The Island archivist, Albert Fulton, speaks of the people as Wardsies and Gonkies. They take their style from their surroundings. Algonquin Island was built in the 1940s on suburban-size lots, so people there tend to stay on their own property and visit each other more or less in the manner of suburbanites. Ward's, on the other hand, began much earlier as a tent city, and the houses are crowded together – it's something like a summer camp that lasts all year. In both communities there's a level of trust among neighbours that recalls the mainland Toronto of two generations ago. Few doors are locked. One longtime Gonkie told me that if she wants to borrow a cup of flour from her neighbours, and the neighbours are out, she goes in, gets it, and leaves a note. "I would be shocked and upset if I found their door locked." Sometimes she and her husband come home and find a note saying a friend has used their dryer. A mainlander might call that an invitation to theft, but burglary almost never happens. One reason is that a stranger approaching an Island house at almost any time of the day or night would probably be noticed by half a dozen neighbours.

As for the question of ownership, a crucial matter to most of us, Liz Amer provides the most persuasive explanation. Her grandmother and great-aunt came to Ward's around 1919, rented a tent site, and built a cottage. Liz started spending summers there as a child and became a year-round Islander in 1953, when she was fifteen. She's been there ever since, through floods and Hurricane Hazel and the demolitions and the Day of the Bridge (she led the negotiations with the sheriff); for six years she was a member of city council, representing the ward that includes the Island. "I always know," she said in a book about the Island a few years ago, "where I can go to get a cup of sugar or a vise grip. If I need a dress made, a pipe threaded, or if I need to know something about geology, there is always someone I can telephone. Sometimes I feel as if I own this community. I don't, but it's as if it belongs to me and I certainly feel as if I belong to it. It is the opposite of 'alienation.'" There are many definitions of ownership; the Islanders have invented one of the best.

9

Downtown North York

THE MOST CASUAL VISITOR could tell that there was something radically wrong with the North York Performing Arts Centre when it opened in 1993. For one thing, someone had put it in the wrong place. The address is 5040 Yonge Street, but it stands a long way west of the Yonge Street sidewalk, forlorn and isolated on the far side of a messy parking lot. The structure itself, with its lumpish shapes coated in beige granite, is no more impressive than the site. It has no windows, no balconies, no terraces, nothing to suggest the pleasures to be found within (they include a good theatre and a superb concert hall). It makes the O'Keefe Centre, a downtown theatre that no one has ever called elegant, look like a Renaissance palace. Can this ungainly object be the work of Eberhard Zeidler, the architect of the Eaton Centre and Ontario Place, one of the most talented designers in Canada?

Clearly, something unfortunate happened at the civic core of North York, the largest of the five suburban municipalities clustered around Toronto and the one that straddles the northern extension of Yonge, the main commercial street of the old city. The exterior of the arts centre, renamed the Ford Centre for the Performing Arts after the automobile company made a late but significant donation, is the architectural equivalent of a major traffic accident. A visitor's first instinct is to ask what in the world caused it, and the answer turns out to be as complicated as history and as subtle as human longing.

All towns of any size eventually realize that public spaces are vital to their psychological well-being, which in turn is crucial to their economic health. Ever since the opening of Nathan Phillips Square, this impulse has been one of the organizing principles of the Toronto region. What the citizens require from their politicians and planners is the creation of places that have meaning for the people who use them. North York failed, and though the immediate causes of failure are local and specific, they carry important lessons for every suburb that hopes someday to transform itself from a collection of private dwellings and private businesses into a community with a satisfying identity. One lesson is that the process is more difficult than anyone might imagine. Another is that grandeur doesn't work.

Zeidler and the $48 million entertainment complex are the victims of municipal grandiosity, ad hoc planning, the recession that began in the late 1980s, and several unhappy accidents. Together these forces damaged not only the Zeidler building but all of North York's "downtown," the place Mayor Mel Lastman once predicted would become "the most modern, beautiful downtown core of anywhere in the world."

Lastman, who was elected in 1972 and has served longer than any other mayor in Metropolitan Toronto, believes passionately that North York, being a "city," should naturally have a downtown – as John Barber noted in *The Globe and Mail* in March, 1995, "He came to the mayoralty with the intention of transforming North York from a bedroom community into a real city. And that, after a fashion, is just what he did." Perhaps the word "downtown" was Lastman's first mistake, because it implies huge buildings similar to those in the core districts of big cities. It can lead to the creation from scratch of a dense and imposing centre that may be only superficially related to the people around it.

Usually a downtown section develops in concentric circles as the city grows: a town of 50,000 or even 25,000 will have an identifiable centre, which will grow steadily larger with the population. North York developed in reverse. The people gathered together, became committed to their lives in a bedroom suburb, and then tried to carve out a core that would move them toward cityhood. In the 1970s, when North York addressed this issue, it already had more than half a million people.

There are many models of city squares around the world, good and bad, but hardly anyone knows how to create one from scratch. The greatest, like the Piazza San Marco in Venice, usually result from the accretion of decisions made over centuries by a disparate collection of people – in the case of San Marco, they included bishops, architects, dukes, artists, and property developers. The worst downtown centres are usually the result of a single mind or a single committee. Architectural critics often cite Nelson Rockefeller's monument, the monotonous, blank-faced Mall in Albany, as the classic example of an urban centre gone wrong. Robert Hughes, in *The Shock of the New*, compares it to Nazi buildings and calls it "the scariest example" of intimidating architecture.

Success in this enterprise demands a balance between large scale and intimacy, between the big building that acts as a powerful symbol and the intimate spaces that are right for drinking coffee, buying a suit, or just sitting in the sun. At North York nothing so horrible as the Albany Mall has been built, but there are few intimate spaces that seem to work and no buildings that have established themselves as symbols of the community that created them.

At various times North York council has authorized elaborate plans, but in the end the main decisions have been made by seizing apparently attractive opportunities as they presented themselves. Lastman and his council had a wish list (including a library and a theatre) and they tried to satisfy it whenever the chance arose. In retrospect their decisions appear to have been shaped more by ego and self-delusion than by a coherent sense of how the community might develop. The result is a cluster of overly ambitious buildings that are stylistically uneven, lacking in human scale, unrelated to the streets around them, and badly sited. You could stand in what purports to be the core of it all, Mel Lastman Square, for a long time before the word "planning" entered your head.

NORTH YORK SET OUT to create what is essentially a strip development, but on a much higher level, figuratively as well as literally. In the 1970s, Lastman and his planners began to focus their attention on "the Yonge Street corridor," a few blocks between Sheppard Avenue and Finch Avenue. In the 1980s, over the objections of residents living in bungalows only a block or two away, they rezoned the corridor for high density.

Earlier, in 1971, the North York Board of Education head-quarters designed by Mathers & Haldenby had become the first major public building on the strip. Today it remains the best-looking structure on the strip and the one building no one complains about. It has a comfortable relationship with the sidewalk, like a real city building, and its chocolate-coloured brutalism holds up better than many designs from that period. It might have provided a model for what came after, but it didn't. Instead, North York's downtown seems to have been more influenced by another building, the spectacularly ill-fated City Hall that Adamson Associates designed in 1978.

Cost is the first thing people mention about the City Hall. At one point there was loose talk of spending $80 million, an idea that died as soon as the voters heard about it. The building that went up cost only $16 million but turned out to be no bargain. Just about everything that could go wrong did. The glass walls make it look like a solar building, but it faces east instead of south. And it feels more like a lobby than a building. Even after major renovation it remains oddly tentative, a preface with no book: you enter, you look for the heart of the enterprise, and before you find it you're going out the back door. The real building never starts.

After the city hall had been in use for a little while, nobody had time to worry about design. They were too busy complaining about practical problems, such as overcrowding. At first glance it looked spacious, but much of the space was deployed uselessly, in great high-ceilinged rooms and halls shaped like wedges of a pyramid. At desk level, everyone felt cramped. Then something worse happened: they began to feel wet, too. The roof sprang a multitude of leaks, and at one point several hundred buckets were being used to catch the water. North York sued two contractors and the architects; eventually the cracks were sealed. In the late 1980s the city added a new wing and made other changes, and the council and staff moved into more comfortable quarters. Then the water started splashing down again – this time on the mayor's desk. A 1990 newspaper story quoted Glenn Garwood, the director of civic projects: "The water would have to go to the mayor's office, of all places. I've had to put up with a lot of embarrassment over this." The building remains an embarrassment.

North York's major architectural event of the 1980s, the $250 million City Centre, equipped with a carillon sometimes called "Mel's Bells," isn't an embarrassment. But it's no ringing success either. After an open competition North York granted Phil Roth's Avro development firm the right to create a shopping, hotel, and office complex in return for providing a public library and a community centre. The design, by Raymond Moriyama, the architect of the Scarborough Civic Centre and many other major projects, looked good on paper, a humming commercial enterprise that would animate a square otherwise devoted to government. The result was disappointing. The shopping mall never quite came to life, partly because it didn't attract glamorous or noteworthy stores at the beginning and partly because it ran into the late-1980s recession just at the moment when it should have been drawing customers away from other malls. The hotel on the north side, Novotel ("the soul of Europe in the heart of North York," one of its 1987 advertisements said) feels cramped and anonymous. Only the public library works well. It's messy, and – spread over seven floors – less than ideally convenient, but it's full of life, and appears to be better than the stores at pleasing its clientele. It has the same pleasantly jumbled feeling that Moriyama achieved in midtown Toronto with his Metropolitan Toronto Reference Library at Yonge Street and Asquith Avenue.

In the summer of 1989, when Mel Lastman Square opened, south of the City Centre, the Toronto *Star* reported: "Lastman, choking back emotion, said he could not explain how proud and moved he was to have the square named in his honor." As a personal tribute it may be satisfying, but as a public square it feels cluttered and incoherent, with its waterfall, seven-hundred seat amphitheatre, wedding chapel, garden court, skating rink, and Lastman's foot-high signature etched in concrete. Its main virtue is that it provides the ceremonial entranceway that the City Hall badly lacked for many years. The City Hall no longer looks as much like an architectural afterthought as it did.

By the time Lastman Square was finished, North York was preparing for a far grander development, just to the south. The Ontario government had bought a ten-acre site for a courthouse but in the end decided not to build. Ontario Hydro then acquired about three-quarters of the land for a new regional headquarters, and formed a partnership with the Canadian Imperial Bank of Commerce (CIBC). They planned three towers, two of them thirty storeys high, one of them twenty-five, with plenty of room for retail, the whole project to be designed by Fedor Tisch of the Webb Zerafa Menkes Housden Partnership, the architect responsible for Scotia Plaza in downtown Toronto.

And that's why the arts centre stands where it stands and looks as it does: it was supposed to fill the remaining quarter of the old courthouse site, on land Lastman had persuaded the Ontario government to give North York. The Hydro-CIBC project was designed to wrap around the arts centre, to its east and south, which would have hidden most of Zeidler's building from the street. Driving past, people would have seen the marquee of the arts centre with its blazing lights, fitted snugly among taller buildings. Zeidler's blank walls make sense only when we understand that they were designed to face other blank walls. He didn't make a good-looking building because nobody was going to look at it.

But Ontario Hydro faltered, in this as in many other ways. It first put the project on hold, and eventually canceled it. At this writing, everything remains ready, from the architectural drawings to the building permits, but nobody wants to build. One day, if another real-estate boom materializes, it may go up. By the mid-1990s North York civil servants were saying in private that they hoped a Hong Kong Chinese billionaire would take an interest. In Toronto, Hong Kong money has become a significant presence, but dreams of Hong Kong money have become even more pervasive.

As late as February 6, 1992, Lastman remained wildly over-confident, the greatest local booster of them all. "Rome wasn't built in a day, but North York is," he said, according to the official text of his press conference. "We have many success stories here today." Later he added, "Through sound financial management and long-term planning, North York has given a model of growth in tough times. . . . We are on top . . . and we like it on top." Seldom have unhappy accidents made the words of a municipal politician sound so hollow so soon.

10

Vaulted Ambition

ALL ARCHITECTURE runs the risk of looking irrelevant when the culture around it changes, but bank buildings suffer more than most. Half a century ago, everyone agreed that the design of a bank had to express the authority of tradition. It had to be respectable and solid, never giddy or faddish. But at some point in the 1960s banks transformed their way of doing business and soon began transforming their architecture as well. They abandoned their quasi-official role as the conservative curators of our money and became an aggressive wing of retailing.

In 1955, respectably employed, I visited a Greek temple around the corner from my office and asked my bank manager to lend me $250 for a visit to London and Dublin, which I saw as part of my education and he saw as a pleasure trip. He of course turned me down. "*I'm* not going to lend you money for your *holidays*," he said. Ten years later, his bank and all others began begging me to go into debt for my holidays, for a red convertible, or for any damn thing that might take my fancy. People were no longer encouraged to think that a penny saved was a penny earned. Bank advertising delivered a new message: a penny borrowed is a penny enjoyed. When that happened, banks changed their appearance. They no longer looked like temples and began to imitate the style of cellophane cookie packages, with large glass windows, bright logos, and advertising that promised infinite pleasure. Money is fun!

That was bad news for the banks designed by John Lyle, a Toronto architect whose buildings were praised through the first half of this century and frequently ignored or disfigured during the second. Lyle was an imaginative fellow, and highly conscious of changing styles in architecture. He liked urging his fellow architects to move beyond the nineteenth-century manner that dominated the city during much of his career. He wanted to absorb and use both historical forms and the new ideas from Europe – though he was anxious not to produce replicas of the "slab-sided box outlines" that appeared in Germany and France in the 1920s and 1930s. He hoped Canada would produce a distinctive national architecture, true to our surroundings; sometimes his buildings used stylized carvings of Canadian wildlife in an Art Deco format.

When it came to designing banks, fun was no part of Lyle's aesthetic. As a result, he symbolizes a problem now confronting those who want to preserve Toronto's architectural past. Most people believe in saving remnants of historic architecture, and we tend to think we know which buildings we should preserve. We have developed platoons of experts who can restore them. But we're not at all sure how we (and our grandchildren) can give these buildings a place of permanent value in a world for which they were not designed. Old architecture may be easier to preserve than to use.

In 1894, a year after the Columbian Exposition in Chicago created a North American fashion for Beaux-Arts design, John Lyle began his studies at the Ecole des Beaux-Arts in Paris, the Vatican of Neo-Classical style. Years later, back in Canada, he made a profession of adapting the most evocative ideas of Greek and Roman architecture. He knew all along what post-modern architects and their patrons have relearned in the last generation: ancient forms, properly understood and appropriated, can charge modern buildings with powerful symbols. On his Royal Alexandra Theatre in 1907 Lyle put the elegant stone parapet that remains one of King Street's enduring architectural pleasures. Ten years later he was one of the architects who made Union Station into a monument of Classical Revival, with its towering entrance colonnade and its Great Hall, still the biggest room in Canada and one of the most elegant (though it's been defiled by clumsy signs and advertising). During much of his life Lyle kept busy designing banks. Patricia McHugh, in *Toronto Architecture: A City Guide,* called him "the architectural master of the Canadian branch bank."

With the passing years, as he shifted from Neo-Classical to Art Deco and Art Moderne, Lyle seems never to have lost his poise. He regarded history as his best friend and most useful tool, but since his death in 1945 history has betrayed him by obscuring his carefully made images and cluttering his elegant spaces. It has made similar fashion victims of other architects who dedicated large parts of their careers to banks. Well-designed little branches by Lyle and his contemporaries now look awkward and isolated in the middle of retail strips whose styles articulate a different age. Lyle's Dominion Bank at Yonge and Gerrard Street, for instance, retains its delicate shape, but now it's surrounded by the chaos of Yonge Street and its image is distorted by its own signs; a building praised when it went up in 1930 gets hardly a glance from people walking past it in the 1990s. Its future is less than secure, and the same can be said for many of the fifty-five financial buildings on the Toronto Historical Board designated list.

The red-brick Toronto-Dominion Bank at 2169 Queen Street East (at Lee Avenue, in the Beach) provides a rather melancholy example. Lyle designed it in 1911 as a branch of the Dominion Bank, and in the context of the Beach district it's an ancient structure as well as a nicely proportioned example of Edwardian Classicism – it was the first bank I ever used, in the 1940s, and even then it was being crowded by the commercial signage that surrounded it. The T-D should be thanked for keeping it, but just to stay alive the building has had to become something Lyle could hardly have imagined: its east-side windows have been enlarged to make the interior bright and welcoming, and the green-and-white T-D logo now dominates the facade. Advertising signs have a way of making us blind to everything but themselves, which is of course their function. Don't look at the architecture, they say, look at what we're selling. At Queen and Lee the old building has become part of the present by obliterating much of its past.

A MORE BIZARRE FATE has befallen the Commercial Bank of the Midland District, constructed in the 1840s at 15 Wellington Street: it has been transformed into a monument to itself. Designed by William Thomas (a virtuoso architect of Victorian Toronto, the designer of St. Lawrence Hall and St. Michael's Cathedral), the Midland District Bank was a gloriously assertive piece of Greek Revival architecture, its limestone facade six bays wide and three storeys high, with six cut-stone piers. When no longer required as a bank, it became the headquarters of the Clarkson Gordon accounting firm.

In 1963, after Walter Gordon left the firm and became federal finance minister, he told some of the modern history of the building in his foreword to Eric Arthur's book about Toronto, *No Mean City*. Gordon mentioned that Arthur had asked him to write the foreword some years earlier, and had said he would be including photographs of 15 Wellington Street West. "Shortly after our conversation, the building was inspected and found to be unsafe. We were ordered to vacate it. Some of my partners thought the building should be demolished to make way for a more modern structure. Others felt this might spoil Professor Arthur's book on which he had been working for some years. They said if I were to write the Foreword, the only decent thing for us to do would be to renovate the building. This argument prevailed and the old Commercial Bank building at 15 Wellington Street West has been completely rebuilt from the inside out. It was a costly undertaking.... Now it will be preserved for many years." Gordon said that his former partners should be glad of this decision, since "there cannot be many chartered accountants who, in Professor Arthur's words, occupy 'A truly fine building which cannot help but evoke thoughts of Greece and of Byron, Shelley, Keats and others.'"

But the building's future was not as Gordon imagined. In 1972 Clarkson Gordon sold it. In the 1980s, when BCE Place was being planned on the site, the developers undertook to preserve the old bank. They fulfilled their promise by taking apart the facade and a couple of rooms and rebuilding them inside the new atrium between Wellington and Front. They changed it from architecture into indoor sculpture. Like the ten nineteenth-century facades they also preserved as a "historic precinct" on the Yonge Street side of BCE Place, the Commercial Bank has been reduced to a fragment of the past – like one of the chunks of old Toronto buildings scattered around the Guild Inn sculpture park in Scarborough. The Commercial Bank facade that once spoke with glorious authority is now merely a nice diversion for people hurrying through the atrium.

This raises the question: Is architecture that has largely lost its purpose still architecture? Is it worth saving merely as a memorial? I think so. As sculpture it's probably more interesting than anything that would have been made for that space. As history it's merely a shadow, but a shadow is better than nothing.

My preservationist views on these matters were shaken by another work of historic reclamation at BCE Place. The developers also promised to save an even more notable piece of history, the old Bank of Montreal at the northwest corner of Front and Yonge. This is one of the loveliest buildings of nineteenth-century Canada, and embodies as much history as any commercial structure in the city. Frank Darling, whose career as a major Toronto architect stretched over something like half a century, designed it (with his then partner, S. George Curry) in the epochal year 1885, when the Riel rebellion was defeated and the Canadian Pacific Railway reached Vancouver. This was to be the bank's Toronto headquarters, and Darling made it an exuberantly rococo celebration of an expanding nation: he gave it Corinthian pilasters at the door, a richly detailed octagonal-shaped interior, and a blizzard of visual allegories spelled out in stone and stained glass. I've always liked to imagine that this was the bank that inspired the most famous of Stephen Leacock's essays, "My Financial Career," about the poor fellow who is so terrified by the act of opening his first account that he inadvertently withdraws all the money he has just deposited and, trying to leave, walks into the vault. Certainly this was the most intimidating bank in Toronto in the late 1880s, when Leacock began teaching in the city.

We can thank BCE Place for saving the building. Today, seeing its once-imposing bulk reduced to the size of a dollhouse by the towers to the north of it, we understand at a glance what has happened to architectural scale in Toronto during the last century. Beyond that, however, BCE Place has done us no favours at all. If we approach the building we discover that it's no longer a bank. We can't enter between those Corinthian pilasters; the entrance is now an emergency exit of the Hockey Hall of Fame. To enter Darling's rococo gem we must go far into BCE Place, take an escalator to the underground level, walk some more, and then pay $7.50 to enter a hell of noisy, logo-infested consumerism. We can visit the Coca-Cola Rink Zone or the Toronto *Sun* Great Moments Zone and revel in ancient videos and relics of games past, the sounds of cheering crowds thrashing the air around us.

Only when we have made our way through this chaos can we get back up to the old bank. There we discover that the interior, its fixtures exquisitely restored, has become the Bell Great Hall. It contains leather chairs, where we can sit in a club-like atmosphere and listen to ancient recordings of Foster Hewitt broadcasting games. There's a row of computer terminals on which we can learn about hockey history. The vault, where Leacock's hero may have strayed, is now Lord Stanley's Vault, containing the original Stanley Cup. From here we can't go directly to the street but must again leave the bank, go downstairs, and escape through a world-class parent trap, a store crowded with more hockey kitsch than you ever knew existed. The building has been preserved, at the cost of radically distorting its meaning and function. Short of destruction, it would be hard to imagine a more hideous fate for Frank Darling's design.

The early 1990s also brought a bank restoration that was as satisfying as the Bank of Montreal's was dismaying. At 205 Yonge Street, on the woebegone commercial strip across from the Eaton Centre, the Toronto Historical Board installed its headquarters in a perfect location, Edward J. Lennox's 1906 Bank of Toronto building. Lennox was one of the great men of his era in Toronto, the designer of the Old City Hall, the King Edward Hotel, and that magnificent folly, Casa Loma. He accepted the Yonge Street assignment as a chance to adapt the Beaux-Arts style to a narrow lot on a busy street, and produced a building of great charm and ingenuity. Beaux-Arts design always involved exaggeration of classical models. Lennox pushed the style farther than most, stopping just short of parody.

The owners were no doubt grateful for his work in the beginning, but their successors lost sight of Lennox's purpose. As Neo-Classicism slipped from favor, the Bank of Toronto (after 1958 it was the Toronto-Dominion Bank) could no longer remember why banks wanted to be elegant in the first place. The managers destroyed the proportions by lowering the ceiling; they took out the skylights, applied layers of linoleum over the marble mosaic floor (which the restorers, miraculously, found intact), and otherwise proved themselves ill-equipped to maintain the history left in their care. A few years ago a team of architects set to work, and eventually gave the building back to the city much as it must have been when Lennox completed it.

Unfortunately, the Toronto Historical Board can occupy only one bank. Perhaps a few others can become museums. The Darling and Pearson 1905 Canadian Bank of Commerce at 197 Yonge Street (south of the Historical Board, just across the park where a plaque commemorates the Colonial Tavern) is now owned by the city; it may become, if the good times roll again, a performing-arts space. Elsewhere in Toronto, as in other cities, there are scores of banks either waiting for restoration or approaching the day when they'll require it. They need to be used as well as preserved, and finding ways to make them workable again will require ingenuity. It's worth the effort. Toronto has always been obsessed with banks, and the bank buildings in our past say as much about our aspirations as anything we have made. It would be unfair to leave them marooned by history.

11

Home on the Grange

HANDED DOWN FROM generation to generation, shaped and reshaped by its owners and their times, a single tract of land can reflect the unfolding identity of a whole city. The Dundas Street West property on which the Art Gallery of Ontario sits, between the dreary corporate monoliths of University Avenue and the exhilarating chaos of Chinatown, is such a place. Over two centuries, history has chosen this site as the theatre for successive dramas of local self-definition, from the embryonic version of the Family Compact at the close of the eighteenth century to the grandest and most opulent party staged by the Toronto financial world near the end of the twentieth.

One recent drama was scripted by New Democratic Party politicians at Queen's Park. In 1992, still fairly fresh in office, still enchanted by their own socialist-populist rhetoric, still firm in the belief that they knew better than anyone about nearly everything, the New Democrats decided that the art gallery was an elitist institution, out of touch with the people of Ontario. Accordingly, the government not only cut the gallery's funds but also appointed a commission to make the AGO more representative of the public. As a result, the gallery closed for six months and cut its staff. It survived that burst of government hostility, and the commission's report was swiftly forgotten, but the controversy carried a peculiar echo of the moment when this site made its first appearance in history. Then, too, the underlying theme was elitism, but the issue was the government's attempt to create rather than displace an elite.

Early in the life of Upper Canada, in the 1790s, Governor John Graves Simcoe decided the colony required a landed aristocracy. In his view, the recent American Revolution was partly the result of Britain's failure to reproduce, in the Thirteen Colonies, the class system of Britain. He wanted to make Upper Canada the "image and transcript of Britain," and even dreamt of creating hereditary titles. He began by making large gifts of land to members of the government. In 1798 one such gift went to Robert Gray, the solicitor general: Park Lot Thirteen, a forest to the west of York. It comprised a wide swath of the land that now lies between Queen Street on the south and Bloor Street on the north.

Gray never had the chance to develop his property. In 1804, just thirty-two years old, he drowned in a storm on Lake Ontario. His will left Park Lot Thirteen to two cousins, but instead his executors sold it, in 1808, to pay Gray's debts. The buyer, at £350, was D'Arcy Boulton Junior, a young lawyer and a member of what would later be described by a political enemy as "one of the most unprincipled families of the Tory compact." The Boultons were to own this land for two generations.

Perhaps they demonstrated their lack of principle in acquiring it. Certainly D'Arcy Boulton Senior, the new solicitor general, was involved in settling Gray's estate, and therefore knew precisely how his son could buy the land. D'Arcy Senior had left England a few years earlier, his affairs clouded by an unresolved bankruptcy. Like other colonial officials, he saw nothing wrong in using his official position to help his family or himself.

The purchase of Park Lot Thirteen helped make the Boultons prosperous; over seven decades they sold off parcels of land for many times the original price. Still, there is no proof that the sum D'Arcy Junior paid was unconscionably low. In 1808 the people of York were numbered in the low hundreds and future prosperity was by no means guaranteed – it wasn't until 1828 that the population exceeded 2,000. And the ruling elite that has gone into history as the Family Compact was still in its infancy. This midget oligarchy, based on the belief that a British-style hierarchy could be imposed on a raw rural society, was made up – as the historian W. Stewart Wallace once put it – "of men, some well-born, some ill-born, some brilliant, some stupid, whom the caprices of a small provincial society, with a code all its own, had pitchforked into power." Its enemies saw the compact as a monolith set permanently in place. In fact, like the Toronto elite of the late twentieth century, it was highly unstable. It changed constantly, frequently waged war with itself, and often stood on shaky financial ground – as the story of Park Lot Thirteen demonstrated.

Among these schemers and social climbers, the Boultons were busy and eager but not remarkably distinguished. William Lyon Mackenzie, who hated the Family Compact, seems to have held the Boultons in particular disdain. In 1834 he compared the Family Compact to a gigantic, evil tree spreading itself over Upper Canada, throwing its shadow over the country, soaking up wealth that should rightfully go to honest workmen: "Look up, reader, and you will see the branches – the Robinson branch, the Powell branch, the Jones branch, the Strachan branch, the Boulton twig, & c." That was a sharp, well-aimed poke. The Boultons, for all their eminence, may have been no more than a twig on the tree of local aristocracy, and in the 1830s most of the other names were indeed more substantial. But only the Boultons left a monument that will endure into the twenty-first century, a handsome, red-brick Georgian house that is now one of the four oldest buildings in Toronto.

D'Arcy Junior built it in 1817-18, in the style that had become familiar in England during the Georgian period, an elegant echo of the sixteenth century buildings of Andrea Palladio. It had a solid, horizontal format, two storeys beneath a central pediment with a round window. Boulton named it The Grange, after the family's ancestral house in England. Eventually he and his friends made it notorious as the symbol of a smug colonialism, the first private house in Ontario that conveyed a clear political message: British aristocratic power is good, democracy not so good. For years, people could reveal their politics by the tone of voice in which they uttered the words "The Grange."

D'Arcy Junior enlarged his property by buying some adjoining land and then began selling it off. He made the neighbourhood more attractive by giving the city a plot for a farmer's market and by donating another piece to the Church of England, to be used for the Church of St. George the Martyr on John Street. That gift also improved Boulton's home: his view from the south porch of The Grange was nicely focused by the church's Perpendicular Gothic tower (the tower still stands, but most of the church was destroyed by fire in 1955). Boulton's largest transaction permanently affected the shape of the city. In 1828, Rev. (later Bishop) John Strachan, the leader of the Church of England in the colony, assembled property for the new University of King's College, paying Boulton £1,300 for fifty-one acres stretching north to Bloor Street. That land eventually was transferred to the University of Toronto; it made the university, forever after, the major property owner in central Toronto.

The city was slowly moving westward. D'Arcy Junior, in the period 1832-1845, sold twenty packages of land near The Grange for more than £2,600. When he died in 1846 he still owned The Grange itself, along with twenty acres, but that remnant soon became the subject of a dispute that threw another shadow over the reputation of the Boultons.

D'Arcy Junior left The Grange to his widow, who soon passed it on to her son, William Henry. He in turn put it in trust for himself and Harriette Mann Dixon, whom he was soon to marry. The reason for that transfer soon became evident: William Henry was in serious financial trouble. His law firm, like his grandfather's in England half a century before, was bankrupt, with nearly £50,000 in liabilities. His creditors tried to seize The Grange and its property, but the trust kept it in the hands of the Boultons.

The rebellion of 1837 began the long process of limiting the Family Compact's control over the affairs of Upper Canada, but The Grange continued to be a seat of some political power. William Henry Boulton represented Toronto in the Legislative Assembly of Canada for eleven years, and served as mayor from 1846 to 1849. George Brown, no friend of Boulton or any other

Tory, judged him harshly. In 1847 Brown wrote in his new paper, the *Globe*: "His manner of speaking is boyish – the kind of half-joking, half-doubting style which a privileged, petted young man is apt to adopt among his seniors." He found Boulton "an energetic, sharp, ambitious young man – but without principle, or steadiness of purpose, or extent of mind to qualify him to sit in Parliament." He did acknowledge, however, that Boulton had the good sense not to speak often in the legislature. Eventually Boulton was defeated in his last run for the legislature and again in his last attempt to be re-elected as mayor. His death in 1874 opened the way for another chapter in The Grange's history.

BOULTON'S WIDOW, HARRIETTE, remarried the following year. Her new husband, Goldwin Smith, was an exotic figure in the young Dominion of Canada. A fifty-two-year-old English bachelor of excellent connections and considerable learning, he had been Regius professor of modern history at Oxford from 1858 to 1866 and then briefly a professor at Cornell University. He had moved to Toronto in 1871. Writing to a friend, he said his marriage was "a union for the afternoon and evening of life." He joined his new wife in The Grange and dwelt there uxoriously for his last thirty-five years, maintaining its position as an outpost of empire. As in the 1830s, The Grange reflected the profound belief of the Toronto leadership class that whatever was good in Canada was essentially British.

His busy pen and the money he invested in magazines like the *Bystander* and the *Week* made Smith the best-known intellectual in Toronto, sometimes called "the Sage of The Grange." He also operated behind the scenes, promoting political causes and writing anonymous editorials for the *Mail*. British connections continued to provide most of his intellectual nourishment, but he became famous for his belief that Canada's future lay with the United States. A liberal in the Manchester free-trade tradition, he favoured commercial union with the U.S. and dreamt happily of the day when Canadians would unite with Americans to create one English-speaking nation within the Anglo-Saxon tradition. His personal dreams were equally grand.

Those who heard his expansive private conversation at The Grange sometimes came away with the idea that he saw himself as a potential president of the continental union he believed he was helping create.

Smith wrote books on subjects ranging from Irish political history to the life of Jesus Christ, but toward the end of his career he realized that he had produced nothing of permanent value. The founder of *Saturday Night* magazine, Edmund E. Sheppard, once said of him, "He is a disappointed man; he thinks that with his abilities he should be filling a much greater place in the world's affairs." Smith came to believe that his literary failure was Canada's fault. He wrote that after he settled in Toronto, "my life as a literary man in the higher sense of the term was at an end. My Oxford dreams of literary achievement never were or could be fulfilled in Canada. Canadians who seek literary distinction, as some have done, not in vain, go to England." He was the spiritual ancestor of all those contemporary Canadian artists who insist that their failures are due to Canada's chronic lack of interest in talent.

Smith seems to have expected that French Canada would shrink to insignificance or disappear. In any case, his refusal to concern himself with its future limited his national influence, and his intense suspicion of Roman Catholics, the Irish, non-whites, and Islam ("not a religion of humanity") have posthumously transformed him from a liberal intellectual into a bigot. His pronounced anti-Semitism makes particularly painful reading today. As Gerald Tulchinsky of Queen's University wrote in 1990, "he was an outspoken Jew-hater, one of the most prominent of his day in the English-speaking world." Smith particularly disliked Benjamin Disraeli – a "contemptible trickster and adventurer. He couldn't help it because he was a Jew." He nourished for many years a grudge against Disraeli for satirizing the young Smith in his 1870 novel, *Lothair,* as a sycophant and a man of "restless vanity and overflowing conceit."

In *Candid Chronicles,* a 1925 book of memoirs, the Toronto journalist Hector Charlesworth recalled that Smith not only wrote articles condoning Russian pogroms but also liked to suggest in private conversation that the rite of circumcision should be extended to include sterilization. Charlesworth noted the happy irony that in the 1920s Smith's Grange Park was the chief playground of the children of Russian and Polish Jews who had settled in the district nearby.

In the first few years of the twentieth century, Smith had many admirers among the young intellectuals of Toronto, notably William Lyon Mackenzie King, the future prime minister, and Vincent Massey, the future governor general. On one occasion Smith invited Massey and two other editors of a university magazine to lunch at The Grange. Massey wrote in his diary on January 1, 1910: "I don't think that from my mind will ever fade the picture of that old scholar sitting, quite bent, in his easy chair with his hands on his stick gazing into the fire.... Outside I could see the elms in the Grange grounds – a calm unviolated retreat in a region of squalor. Within were the stately Georgian apartments with their lofty ceilings and dignified lines. And in the centre of such a setting was the one man in Canada who could occupy it naturally...he is the spirit of stately and graceful simplicity." Smith talked about Gladstone and other great nineteenth-century figures he had known. Half a century later, in his memoirs, Massey wrote: "His manner of living was very rare in the Canada of the day. We were struck by the ritual of his handing the keys of the wine-cellar to the butler, who was asked to bring up a bottle of sherry."

During the Hitler period, both King and Massey (as High Commissioner for Canada in Great Britain) expressed their own anti-Semitism by excluding from Canada as many Jewish immigrants as possible. In 1946, writing in his diary, King recalled Smith's remark that the Jews were "poison in the veins of a community." There was no scandal attached to those views in Smith's day.

At The Grange, Smith was apparently a happy man. "Fortune," he wrote in *Reminiscences,* "made for me almost an England of my own in Canada. The Grange at Toronto, with its lawn and its old elms, is the counterpart in style and surroundings of a little English mansion.... It originally stood outside the city, though now it is in the exact centre. In summer, when the trees are in leaf, nothing is seen from its door but a church spire." The servants lived in four pretty little cottages in the park to the south. In the English way, they stayed with the family more or less forever: when Smith died, in 1910, his butler had been at The Grange for just under fifty-two years. The Grange became the place where eminent visitors to Toronto were entertained. In 1884 Matthew Arnold wrote a thank-you note to Smith: "We often talk of our stay with you and Mrs. Goldwin Smith in that delightful old house at Toronto; we found nothing so pleasant and so like home in all our travels."

Since the Smiths had no children to inherit their property, the future ownership of The Grange was uncertain. In 1902 this delicate point was raised by a visitor, the banker Edmund Walker. Two years earlier, Walker and the painter George A. Reid had founded the Art Museum of Toronto, a title more hopeful than descriptive. They had no building, and for a while they mounted their exhibitions in borrowed space. Walker suggested that The Grange might be bequeathed to the museum as its permanent home, and the Smiths agreed. When Smith died, in 1910, the museum inherited the house and the six remaining acres to the south of it, which have been used as a public park ever since. The museum held its first exhibition there in 1913, and soon began the program of expansion that has continued, off and on, ever since.

Sir Edmund Walker, who has mainly disappeared from public memory, was utterly unlike any major Canadian business executive in the late twentieth century. A self-educated farm boy, he became general manager of the Bank of Commerce at the age of thirty-eight and ran it as president from 1907 until his death in 1924. He was the dominant figure in the founding of the National Gallery of Canada and the Royal Ontario Museum as well as the Art Gallery of Toronto. He could lecture on early Italian painting or the future of Japan. In his youth he learned to identify counterfeit money, which left him with a lifelong interest in printmaking, especially etching; his print collection included Rembrandt and Dürer. For a Canadian, he had an unusual sense of dynasty: he left to his twenty-two grandchildren the family vacation compound he created at Degrassi Point on Lake Simcoe, 220 acres stretching along a kilometre of waterfront; his descendants own it still, and in the 1990s scores of blood relatives meet there in the course of a summer.

Under his supervision, Frank Darling – the much-honoured architect was then in his mid-sixties – designed three long galleries to be attached to the north of The Grange. They opened in 1918, and there, on May 7, 1920, another kind of history was made. A remarkable collection of new paintings went up on Darling's Italianate walls, among them *The Tangled Garden* by J. E. H. MacDonald and *Terre Sauvage* by A. Y. Jackson. This was the first exhibition of the Group of Seven, the opening shot in the campaign that eventually changed not only art in Canada but the Canadian imagination itself. It was the most inspired publicity coup in Canadian cultural history.

The timing was perfect. In the 1920s, Canada made its longest strides toward legal independence, notably at the Colonial Conference of 1926, which for the first time defined Canada and the other dominions as autonomous communities within the British Empire. The Group of Seven, coming together in the first spring of that crucial decade, rode a wave of English-Canadian nationalism.

They also perpetrated a magnificent fraud, permanently installing in the public mind an altogether bogus view of their history. The painters and a few tireless publicists in the press created a self-serving myth of underdog artists fighting for their radical vision against a narrow, conservative society. More than seventy years later, most people believe that the group "provoked the ire of the artistic establishment" (as the 1988 *Canadian Encyclopedia* says) and faced "the inevitable backlash" (as a Toronto *Star* piece said in 1992). In fact, it would be hard to find, in the entire history of art, another school of painters who started out with so many advantages and such enthusiastic support from their country's establishment. The Group's powerful friends ranged from the director of the National Gallery of

Canada, Eric Brown, to the co-founder of the *Canadian Forum,* Barker Fairley. They had a great patron in Dr. James MacCallum and their own number included Lawren Harris, who lived handsomely on income from Massey-Harris, the multinational farm-implements firm.

And, of course, the group was allowed to hold its first exhibit at the Art Gallery of Toronto, the new temple of elite Toronto. The exhibition foreword, apparently written by Harris, said the artists expected "ridicule, abuse or indifference," from collectors tied to commercial fashion, but they held out the hope that "a very small group of intelligent individuals... will welcome and support any form of Art expression that sincerely interprets the spirit of a nation's growth." This aggressive appeal to nationalist snobbery, with its suggestion that patrons identify themselves as an enlightened minority, became part of the style of the group and its admirers.

In later years members of the group often claimed that their first show was greeted with hostility. In 1964 A. Y. Jackson, in his autobiography, *A Painter's Country,* wrote about the 1920 exhibition: "There was plenty of adverse criticism, little of it intelligent. A great deal of it was mere abuse...." But Jackson was just pumping up the myth. As Dennis Reid wrote in 1970 in the catalogue of the Group of Seven exhibition at the National Gallery, the idea that the show was severely attacked in the press "is absolutely false." The reviews were mildly encouraging, never harsh. And there was no question that the Toronto Establishment blessed the group at its birth. In the three-quarters of a century since, no similar organization has begun life within the walls of the AGO.

Frank Darling died in 1923, and his firm, Darling and Pearson, continued to expand the building in his style, finishing new sections in 1926 and 1935. The indoor sculpture court at the core of the building was named the Walker Court, to honour Sir Edmund. Today, two major renovations later, it's still the centre of the building, but it's an inappropriate monument to a busy and purposeful man. It's not much good for showing art and it's too big and unfocused for lectures or concerts. It functions best, perhaps, for occasional grand dinner parties and weddings.

IN ARCHITECTURE, as in the other arts, each generation establishes its legitimacy by destroying its fathers, masking ambition with the rhetoric of progress. This ritual of patricide has seldom been so flamboyantly performed as in the history of the AGO, which has grown through a series of rejections. In building the first version of the Art Gallery of Toronto, Darling and Pearson pretty well ignored the existence of The Grange (whose designer is unknown). John C. Parkin, in the early 1970s, rejected Frank Darling. And in the late 1980s Barton Myers and his colleagues rejected John C. Parkin.

But the building expresses far more than the ideas of a few architects. The persistent denial of the past illustrates something much larger, Toronto's undernourished self-image. Each architect, after all, was performing for clients who wanted a building that reflected themselves and their dreams. What they did not want, clearly, was any reflection of Toronto history.

From the beginning the clients included the public, the artists and the trustees, not all of whom were mainly interested in looking at pictures. Leaders of Toronto society tended to regard the gallery as more a social than a cultural centre, and by the 1950s winning a place on the junior women's committee was one of the greatest social achievements open to a well-connected young Toronto matron. After 1965, when the Art Gallery of Toronto became the Art Gallery of Ontario and turned into a dependency of the provincial government, the architects' body of clients grew to include civil servants and politicians. Few of these people knew much about art or museums, but most of them offered their opinions to the gallery staff. Often they felt vaguely that the AGO wasn't as popular as it should be, and would attract more visitors if it ceased to fuss about collecting art and instead concentrated on crowd-pleasing. They also liked to say that the AGO should fall into line with government "policy" for cultural agencies, though they could rarely enunciate the policy.

Aside from dealing with bureaucratic busybodies and self-important board members, each architect has also dealt with different design problems, the first difference being scale. Each of them has made a bigger and more complex building for a bigger and more complex city.

FRANK DARLING PUT what seemed like a huge building behind a pleasant old mansion. His chosen style was Renaissance Revival, which he used with a cool elegance; he decorated his nicely proportioned galleries with baseboard mouldings in black marble and delicate plaster cornices. He used natural light, admitted gently from overhead to avoid damaging the art. Strolling through his elegant rooms, it was possible to imagine that this public museum, like so many in Italy, had once been a ducal palace. The contents, however, were not what one would find in Italy. The Toronto rich, unlike those in Cleveland and other enlightened cities, showed little interest in buying the Florentine and Venetian masters. The masterworks that hung on Darling's walls tended, more often, to be Dutch – and there were not a great many of those. In fact, the greatest problem of the gallery, then as now, was not its building but its core constituency, the leadership class of Toronto.

During most of the years of the AGO's development, wealthy Toronto people, with rare exceptions, were not deeply interested in buying the sort of art that makes a museum important. They were willing to serve on the board, but at the primary task assigned to them by cultural tradition – collecting pictures that would eventually go onto the gallery walls – they were a dismal failure. In the first half of the century there were no great collectors in Toronto (the city won't know the results of collecting in the second half of the century for some years).

Whatever the priorities of Toronto's leaders in the first few decades of the gallery's life, they did not include The Grange. Darling's design turned its back on The Grange and faced north. By the 1930s, The Grange looked like an outbuilding. Torontonians saw little reason to preserve the physical embodiment of a past that they found only marginally interesting, and The Grange in particular represented a history no one was anxious to celebrate. From the 1920s to the late 1940s, the dominant politician in Canada was Prime Minister William Lyon Mackenzie King, the proud grandson of the radical who had fought the people who were at home in The Grange. History books told us that Mackenzie, in the Rebellion of 1837, had challenged the bad men from England and helped bring responsible government to Canada. Who cared, then, about preserving a house created by would-be aristocrats who ended up on the losing side?

The Grange was left to rot. By the 1950s the gallery's offices and library were housed there, the telephone switchboard jammed under the Boultons' elegant staircase and the bedrooms crammed with desks and filing cabinets. Those in charge showed little interest in even cleaning and painting the building, much less restoring it to the style the Boultons and the Smiths knew. This was the state of things in 1961, when William Withrow became director. Within a few years, he and the trustees were planning a much larger museum, of which The Grange would be an honoured part. Its time had come again: the city was developing historical pride. The Grange reopened to the public in 1973, restored by the preservationist architect Peter John Stokes. It was remade in the style the first Boulton occupants knew in the 1830s, from furniture to table-settings; carpets were woven in England to a pattern from the period, and wallpaper was printed to match fragments found behind plastered-over walls.

THIS NEW SENSE of history did not extend to the expansion of the main buildings that John C. Parkin was then preparing. Parkin had been the young prince of Canadian architecture in the 1950s, having brought back from Harvard a particularly severe form of modernist doctrine. He was a handsome and charming man who gave the impression that he was furiously social-climbing even when he was sitting still and silent. He was the architect as socialite, a road-company version of the original part created by Stanford White in New York late in the nineteenth century. Entertaining in his boxy, modernist Don Mills home, with its Mies van der Rohe chairs and its hotel-lobby atmosphere, he sold himself as he sold modernism – with great flair and boundless ambition. His conversation was smooth, glib, and ingenious. In explaining the virtues of his designs to a reluctant client, he could (as someone once wrote of Vincent Massey) polish a cliché until it shone like an epigram.

In his hands, the legacy of Frank Darling was doomed. Parkin had no interest in the historic buildings of Toronto, and no patience with nostalgia. In the 1960s, in the midst of a furious public controversy, he had argued that Edward J. Lennox's 1899 City Hall should be demolished to make way for the Eaton Centre. After all, he pointed out, Lennox's building was not a particularly good example of Richardsonian Romanesque, and he was unmoved by the argument that it was the best we had. He lost that battle, but he spoke for a powerful faction in the Toronto of his day. Yearning for international status, the city increasingly identified with its American equivalents. It wasn't surprising that it embraced the International Style as imported by Parkin. Nor was it surprising that Parkin's version of the AGO both enclosed and overwhelmed Frank Darling's.

Parkin's two-part extension opened in 1974 and 1977, a set of cold, austere boxes. In almost every way it was a disaster. "Architecture should enliven, ennoble and inspire, and not gratify or glorify the banal," Parkin once wrote. No one would apply any of those words, except the last, to his AGO. It was, first of all, wretchedly planned. Parkin may have wanted to refrain from officiously directing the flow of visitors, but what he provided was incoherence. There was no logic to the relationship of the entrance, the halls, and the galleries. Parkin replaced the easily flowing spaces of the old Darling building with grand openings that led nowhere; it took some of us years to find our way around. Parkin wanted a noncommittal building in which art could make its own statement, but the result was at once baffling and boring. And there was one gigantic gaffe: a grand staircase that led straight to the coat-check room.

Parkin eliminated most of the natural light sources and masked the graceful details of Darling's design with false ceilings and neutral wall-covering, as if baseboards and cornices were ancestral crimes to be hidden. In their place, he was unable to provide any grace of his own. One of modernism's chief glories, delicately proportioned rooms used as a subtle aesthetic statement, was altogether absent. The failure of the building was an emblem of the failure of modernist architecture, which by that point had lost much of its energy and conviction and was going languidly through the motions of its own ideology. It had become a system, and not much more.

Except for the Henry Moore Centre, the self-contained section exhibiting Moore's enormous gift of his own work, there was little that anyone found to admire in the new AGO. One major flaw, the poor quality of the building materials, couldn't be blamed on either John Parkin or the gallery staff. It was the result of a shoestring budget set by the provincial government of the 1970s. That's the reason much of the building was clad in what looked like congealed porridge. William Withrow remarked later that the government made sure that everything, right down to the doorknobs, was "post-office minimal."

Something else was wrong with the Parkin building: it was dated before it opened. It said "modernist," clearly and bluntly, at a moment when cultural buildings all over the world were moving beyond modernism. In 1976, a year before Parkin's second stage opened, the new Citadel Theatre went up in Edmonton, a graceful and airy work of high-tech post-modernism. The architect was Barton Myers – and it was Myers who in 1987 won the competition to enlarge the AGO. Enlarge it and, once again, change it radically.

MYERS MOVED to Los Angeles after winning the competition, and he shared credit for the new AGO with his old Toronto partners; when it opened in 1993, the credit line reflected the building's mixed parentage: "Architects: Barton Myers Architect Inc., Kuwabara Payne McKenna Blumberg Architects – Joint Venture Architects." The partner in charge was Thomas Payne. These architects and their clients (including Withrow, the director emeritus, and his successor, Glenn Lowry) transformed the tone of the whole museum. They tore out Parkin's false ceilings in the old Darling galleries, ripped down Parkin's oatmeal-coloured fabric wall-covering, softened Parkin's lighting. They restored Darling's baseboards and cornices. They abandoned Parkin's near-white walls and began experimenting with crimson, mustard, and other background colours that

Parkin's generation regarded as outlandish. Outside, they erected a forty-six-metre-high decorative tower to make the gallery more prominent on crowded, busy Dundas Street. They placed a glass pyramid over the new entrance hall.

They also eliminated the pretentious ceremonial entrance Parkin had built. According to a 1975 article in *Canadian Architect,* Parkin's goal was to create an inviting facade with "none of the monumental qualities so characteristic of galleries and museums throughout history." He failed, partly because he put a moat-like space between the street and the building. Myers and his partners eliminated the moat and moved the entrance from the middle of the building's front toward the eastern end. But their facade, while much better than Parkin's, was still no triumph. It lacked style and focus, the entrance remained confusing and constricted, and a much-too-large retail outlet was left to dominate the street side.

Clearly, the architects of the 1990s felt about Parkin as Parkin felt about Darling. Wherever they could, they hid his design, and when the new gallery opened it was almost entirely deParkinized. But they did not ignore the history of the site. Their approach was summed up in a remark Payne made during construction: "Most great institutions are built incrementally over time." This truth is central to his generation's view of architecture; denying it was central to Parkin's. The 1993 building expresses one of the paradoxes of post-modernism: in order to advance, architecture must frequently retreat, and must never hesitate to acknowledge the past (except, of course, the immediate past known as modernism – which must be obliterated, if possible).

The long, two-storey Joey and Toby Tanenbaum Sculpture Atrium illustrates this way of thinking. It is the noblest moment in the new AGO, another of the significant public spaces created in Toronto after 1965. It has the focus that the Walker Court spectacularly lacks, and it acts as a kind of architectural anthology, a visual history of the site. The glass south wall looks out onto the old Georgian mansion built by the Boultons, now finally given a place of honour. Frank Darling's 1918 Italianate design, its stone freshly scrubbed, provides the north wall: it's a fragment of Darling's exterior, moved indoors. The west wall and the arching roof recall earlier Myers buildings. And, at the east end of the room, obscured by the bar and the restaurant, we can still catch a glimpse of John C. Parkin's modernism.

Here, and in several other places, the site became more beautiful and inviting than at any time since Goldwin Smith lived in The Grange. Perhaps it will satisfy what Payne has defined as his firm's goal: "buildings that will look just as good fifty years from now . . . as they do today." Given the history of art museums, and this one in particular, that seems uncertain. But, beyond question, the most recent AGO continues the site's tradition by encapsulating Toronto's current idea of itself. In its dreams, the Toronto of the 1990s is open, democratic, pluralistic, and stylish. No other building in the city illustrates that vision as effectively as the Art Gallery of Ontario.

DURING THE LAST sixteen weeks of 1994, 597,127 people came to the AGO to pay fifteen dollars for an hour spent with an unusual exhibition, "From Cézanne to Matisse: Great French Paintings from The Barnes Foundation." The most publicized event in the two-hundred-year history of the site, the Barnes show turned out to be the enactment of a civic ritual. These paintings by European masters, some great and some not, became the basis for an affirmation of Toronto's most intoxicating dreams, a high-culture equivalent of the Blue Jays' World Series victories. It was also a demonstration of the way museums have responded to the environment in which they now must live, and a manifestation of a trend in the merchandising of culture that had been developing over two or three decades.

Those responsible for promoting the arts, and keeping alive the institutions that house and nourish them, have noticed that audiences are less reliable and more demanding than they once were. Many people who might be expected automatically to support the arts have apparently lost the habit. Audiences at symphony concerts, for instance, are shrinking, and growing ominously old. Ordinary good work, in performance or exhibition, has lost much of its appeal. At the same time, the arts have reflected the fragmenting of society. In each art form, audiences have split into smaller groups, most of them isolated from each other. Art, which began as part of religious ritual, has lost much of its ability to produce images and ideas of broad relevance.

Those promoting the arts have responded by emphasizing events that rise above the usual standards and generate excitement. People who wouldn't dream of seeing a film from Taiwan at an ordinary cinema will line up to see one at the Toronto International Film Festival. People who rarely go to the symphony can be coaxed out of their homes if some great virtuoso makes a first, or last, or only, appearance in their city – or if two or three virtuosi perform together for the first time. Increasingly, culture seems to require the aura of a special occasion, and creating that aura has become the goal of every cultural promoter.

All of these tendencies came together at the AGO in 1990 with the arrival from Washington of the new director, Glenn Lowry. The AGO Lowry took over had, in one sense, a glowing future: the new building was in the works. But as an institution it was not firmly established in the mind of the city or the province. Many people, including most of those in a position to influence its future, saw it as dull and marginal. Lowry determined to change its status, and seized on the blockbuster as the means of change.

The blockbuster exhibition was invented by another American cultural promoter, Thomas Hoving, at the Metropolitan Museum of Art in New York in the 1960s, as a way of drawing attention as well as crowds. Lowry and the president of the gallery, Joe Rotman, saw the Barnes exhibit as an event that would capture the attention of Toronto. With great difficulty, they obtained the right to show it in Toronto.

As several critics pointed out, this use of paintings collected by Dr. Albert C. Barnes (1872-1951) was intensely ironic. He would have hated everything about the exhibition in Toronto, as he would have hated its appearances in Washington, Paris, and elsewhere. Barnes was a cranky grievance-collector, but he had a firm idea of how art should be seen: in context, and carefully. In

1922 he put his splendid collection in a building he constructed in suburban Philadelphia, forbade colour reproductions of it, and barred the door to any but dedicated students; he personally decided which potential viewers were serious enough to see it. His will prohibited the lending or touring of his pictures. It was only when the original building was falling apart that a Pennsylvania court finally violated his wishes and permitted a sampling of the pictures to go on a fund-raising tour.

Barnes would have been mortified by the sight of tourists, stuffed into buses, arriving at the AGO to take a one-hour look at some of his Cézannes and Renoirs. He might have been even more upset to realize that he had helped create the atmosphere for this promotion. By making his pictures so hard to see over the years, he had spawned a legend of secrecy that played into the hands of art promoters. In Toronto the $1-million advertising campaign used a slogan that perfectly encapsulated the idea of culture as an event: "Never Before. Never Again." As the exhibition came to an end, in late December, the advertising became urgent: "Miss the Barnes in the next 5 days and you'll miss it forever." John Bentley Mays wrote in *The Globe and Mail* that the advertising campaign was "the real masterpiece here, certainly a cut above most of the paintings on display. . . . "

The AGO presented the Barnes exhibition as, above all, a superb tourist attraction. "Great art is also smart business," Lowry said, and the politicians agreed with him. Premier Bob Rae, whose government had taken a viciously anti-elitist stand against the gallery only two years earlier, was an enthusiastic supporter. His minister of culture, tourism and recreation said that the $3.75 million the government invested in the exhibition was a "component of our provincial tourism strategy." For the most part, Toronto journalists fell into line. As Richard Rhodes said in *Canadian Art* magazine, "The coverage . . . in Toronto was almost entirely about economics. The Monets, Renoirs, Seurats, van Goghs, Picassos and Matisses were spoken of as if they were convertible currency. . . . These pictures were like yachts in a boat show; they had become opportunities to fantasize about wealth and fame and a deluxe lifestyle." In reply the managers of the AGO might ask: What else could we do? We need great events in order to make people notice our museum, and to get great events we must get large crowds. Like museums in many parts of North America and Europe, the AGO came to the conclusion that it had to choose between going into show business and going out of business.

Even the corporate sponsors became part of the Barnes story, greatly enhancing its value as an event. Gluskin Sheff & Associates, a Toronto investment firm, contributed $1 million to cover some of the expenses, the highest sum ever paid by the sponsor of a single event in Canada. In 1994 the firm was ten years old, and a remarkable success; Ira Gluskin and Gerry Sheff had done so well for their clients that (according to the business writer Patricia Best) they had each earned $15 million in 1993.

Gluskin and Sheff decided to spend another $1.25 million to celebrate their gift and their tenth anniversary. They took over the gallery on Monday, September 12, five days before the official opening, and put on the most lavish party in the history of Toronto. The invitations alone cost $200 each (everyone invited got a copy of the $89.95 catalogue in a handmade wooden box) and the flowers $75,000. The 1,700 guests sat beneath an enormous tent erected for the occasion in Grange Park, eating rack of lamb and drinking Pol Roger. Under the tent a bar, forty-four feet long, mahogany-finished, was built for this one night.

An anonymous writer in *Toronto Life* called the party "the symbolic end to the recession" and "a milestone in Toronto society, a coming out for the new power elite" – and indeed, there was a feeling that the evening marked a changing of the guard, though there was no reason to think that this newly constituted compact was any more permanent than the Toronto elites of the past: business and social elites often seem permanent, but experience suggests that they change as quickly as styles in art. *Toronto Life* quoted a "High wasp" who commented: "The old wasps were there, but it wasn't their night." That was a euphemistic way of saying that the evening was a clear public statement of one of the most significant social changes in the history of Toronto, the absorption of a remarkable number of

Jews into the elite of the city – into, that is, the late-twentieth-century equivalent of the Family Compact.

The setting gave this implicit statement a unique emphasis. At The Grange, in Goldwin Smith's time, Jews were not only unwelcome but reviled. Anti-Semitism, then and for generations after, was part of everyday Toronto life. But, beginning in the 1950s, the place of Jews radically changed. People whose grandparents had lived meagre lives in downtown slums, or whose parents had entered Canada over the strenuous objections of bigoted politicians and bureaucrats in Ottawa – these people, by brains and energy, became a vital force in business, the arts, and the professions. Anti-Semitism was not eliminated, but it was defeated on all the important grounds where it was engaged. By the 1980s it was obvious that the Jews of Toronto were more than successful; they were essential. It was hard to imagine how Toronto would function – in medicine, for instance, or the law, or architecture, or literature, or show business, or land development – if Jews in earlier generations had accepted their rejection by respectable Toronto as a final judgment and had gone off to live elsewhere.

At the AGO party, the president of the gallery, Joe Rotman, helped Gluskin and Sheff welcome the guests, who included Sylvia Ostry, Mickey Cohen, Judge Rosalie Abella, David Mirvish, Murray Frum, and Ydessa Hendeles, along with Galen Weston, Ted Rogers, Conrad Black, Ken Thomson, and other members of an older elite. It was a spectacle that would have astonished the Boultons, and would have left Goldwin Smith paralyzed with horror and indignation. For anyone who understood the history of this site, it was an exquisite moment of revenge, worth savouring forever.

WHETHER THEY ADMIRED the Barnes exhibit or not, those who felt connected to the Art Gallery of Ontario would always look back on that autumn as a season in the sun. It was a time when, for once, the AGO was at the centre of the city's thoughts. That was Joe Rotman's intention when he campaigned to bring the exhibition to Toronto. "I saw the Barnes as the basis for the repositioning of the art gallery," he told Ron Graham of *Toronto Life*. "In one fell swoop the Barnes would pull the AGO up to a new level – one that it had never strived for before – in the eyes of the staff, the government, the donors, the public and the outside world." When the show closed and the paintings were packed up, the AGO occupied a new place in the imagination of Toronto. Whether it can hold that place remains an open question.

There were those who imagined that the Barnes exhibition had an even larger meaning for Toronto and its self-image. Perhaps it was, as Christopher Hume argued in the *Star*, "a unique example of success, proof that we don't have to be the backwater we're used to thinking we are." For a few celebratory months, Toronto seemed to join the great cities, where great public events occurred. Once more, Park Lot Thirteen had become the site of Toronto's dreams.

12

Monumental Success

THE GUIDE TO EXHIBITIONS handed out free in the art galleries of Toronto, *Slate,* lists the Morrow Avenue galleries under "downtown," a euphemism that may well mislead innocent strangers. Morrow Avenue is "downtown" only in the sense that it's not in Mississauga, or Hamilton. Otherwise, it's not downtown at all: it's a good five kilometres north-west of the Art Gallery of Ontario. I imagine an innocent tourist noticing in *Slate* that four downtown galleries that sound interesting happen to be on the same street. The tourist hails a taxi and gives the address. The tourist may be surprised when the driver has to look up Morrow on a map – still, what the hell, most cities have incompetent cab drivers. As time passes and the taxi travels through neighbourhoods that look less and less like the sort of place where art lives, the tourist's confidence in the whole project slowly fades.

Even when the taxi turns from Dundas Street West onto somewhere called Morrow Avenue, with ten dollars or so showing on the meter, the surroundings remain bleak. Worn-out factories and tired little houses dominate the local cityscape. This can't be it: what does that guide say again? The first building on Morrow sells drywall, the next sells lumber. But on the roof of the third, the one that backs onto the CNR tracks, there's a hopeful sign, if you happen to look up: a self-portrait of the sculptor John McEwen, silhouetted in steel.

And when the cab turns into the courtyard at 17-23 Morrow, persistence is finally rewarded by something quite wonderful. The buildings surround the visitor and art asserts its unlikely presence. Here are four art galleries, plus a restorer's studio, a framing store, the studios of an industrial designer and a graphic designer, all of them wrapped around an open square that suggests the Industrial Revolution's idea of a medieval courtyard. This is an artistic precinct, west end Toronto's own little Rue des Beaux-Arts. It's also an experiment in micro-urbanism, an exercise in personal town planning.

The Morrow Avenue cluster, built as factory spaces in the style of the late nineteenth century, has been converted to the purposes of the late twentieth century. In recent years this has become familiar architectural alchemy. All over the western world, art has been installed in discarded industrial sites crusted with the grime of generations. Painting and sculpture have found new homes in structures designed mainly for the comfort of machines, structures that the world regarded as unremarkable and even ugly until obsolescence endangered their existence and helped us see the gallant beauty in their battered shells. In the most famous case, the Musée d'Orsay in Paris fills what used to be a gigantic railway station.

The art centre at Morrow Avenue is on a smaller scale, to put it mildly, but it's designed in the same tradition. It carefully respects the old context while creating a new one, so that we experience it as layers of history, veined by time like a slice of ancient rock. A loading dock that leads towards two of the galleries was entirely rebuilt, but it still looks like a loading dock. An elevator shaft has become an outdoor sculpture court, but retains its original shape. The Cor-Ten steel doors to the biggest gallery move easily on their hinges, but they look emphatically industrial. Inside the galleries, gigantic old wooden beams remain exposed, competing in visual power with the sculpture beneath them. The developer has acknowledged the past of the site, leaving in clear view the fading sign that reminds us of a former owner, Canadian Hanson & Van Winkle Co. Limited.

THE ROOTS of the Morrow Avenue art centre can be traced to a town-planning development of the 1960s. When the crowds and noise generated by Honest Ed Mirvish's famous discount house at Bloor and Bathurst Streets enraged his neighbours, Mirvish bought up all their houses and turned a block of Markham Street into a commercial artistic community, Mirvish Village. In the same era, he became a downtown developer by buying the Royal Alexandra Theatre on King Street and several buildings near it. He opened a series of restaurants on the north side of King Street, and in the 1990s built the Princess of Wales Theatre. In each case he followed the old street line and the context of the neighbourhood, so that the Princess of Wales fits snugly into the block and at a quick glance looks as if it might always have been there. Mirvish proved himself a sensitive town planner, much more respectful of the urban environment than non-profit institutions nearby, such as Roy Thomson Hall and the CBC Broadcasting Centre.

At the original site on Markham Street, Mirvish's son established the David Mirvish Gallery and for several years made an astonishing success selling abstract paintings to buyers from all over North America. In one of the basements on that street, on June 7, 1973, Olga Korper, a former art teacher and magazine designer, opened her first gallery. Later she expanded into a whole house, still in Mirvish Village. In 1980 she moved to 80 Spadina Avenue, an old garment-industry building that eventually held some two dozen galleries of radically varying quality, from the wonderful to the dreadful.

Hers was among the best. In the most successful year at that location she grossed about $1 million. By 1988 the rent was going up, the elevator service wasn't all it should be, and she was dreaming of something more ambitious. She talked to other dealers about jointly buying a building, and looked at several sites. Finally she focused her attention on Morrow Avenue, where land speculators had purchased a few vacant industrial buildings a couple of years earlier.

She had never visited Morrow Avenue before, and did not know it existed until a lawyer friend told her he had purchased a chunk of it. There was no reason she should have heard of it. For about a century it had been one of those hundreds of urban streets devoted mainly to the more obscure forms of industry. Frank Morrow, a real estate developer who owned a couple of buildings there, named it after himself in the 1880s. The surrounding district briefly had village status: in 1883 and 1884 it was the Village of Brockton, named for Sir Isaac Brock, and Frank Morrow was a village councillor. In 1884 the council, having failed to agree on how to deal with the municipal debt, submitted to annexation by Toronto, where Morrow was later employed as city assessor. By 1890 Morrow Avenue and the streets nearby were laid out and named.

Early in this century Canada Label & Webbing Co. operated on Morrow Avenue, and in 1914 Canadian Hanson & Van Winkle, makers of industrial brushes, had set up a factory there. Canadian Hanson spread over the site for half a century, then moved on. In 1967 the Marshall Mattress Co. took over the property and stayed there until relocating in the suburbs in 1986.

By 1988, when Korper first saw it, the buildings had that melancholy air of once-busy sites abandoned by history. Junk covered the floors and the ground outside. But when she looked at it she imagined paintings on the walls, sculpture on the floors, gallery assistants sitting at the desks, and clients happily buying art. To purchase the complex, she formed a partnership with seven people who were friends, clients, bridge partners, or all three. The original financial commitment was made in March, 1988, a happy moment in economic history.

Korper and the architect, Kearns Mancini, faced all the usual problems of renovation, and a few extra ones. Squatters came and went: during the rebuilding, an overnight visitor made a bonfire to keep warm and nearly burned the place down. Just about all the plumbing, heating, and wiring had to be replaced, as did all windows and some foundations. Teenagers who lived nearby had come to believe they owned the messy, empty square, and they resented the arrival of a new owner so much that they broke all the new windows on one side of the building; unbreakable plastic replaced them.

The Olga Korper Gallery opened its new space in October, 1989 – just in time for the first bad winter of the recession, when the art business sank into the worst depression anyone could remember. The other art dealers who had expressed interest in owning part of the development now declined, for excellent reasons. Korper says of the people who did invest: "Some of them sort of said, 'I'll give you this money, try not to lose it.' My partners should go down in history as supporting culture. They have not always been pleased with me. It has not been an easy ride for them."

Her problems were of the sort many imaginative developers face, all of them intensely complicated by the recession. The 1988 price of the property was $2 million, and rebuilding plus carrying charges added another $2.5 million. She couldn't get a construction mortgage, since her plan made little business sense, and in the end she had to rely on a demand loan. As it turned out, that was an advantage. "The fall in interest rates saved us. Without that, we would have been a goner. The T-D Bank has been good to me." For years, survival was in question. "There were times when I literally made myself sick. Slowly my subconscious accepted the fact that I was going to survive, no matter what, but it was not going to be easy. It's not courage. It's stamina and stubbornness beyond words."

In truth, the recession made an eccentric idea look altogether foolish. Her fellow dealer (and later, for a while, her tenant), Fela Grunwald, remembers: "There were a lot of people who thought that she couldn't do it. After being her neighbour at 80 Spadina, I wasn't one of them. Olga makes things happen through sheer will, energy, and fortitude."

For a while there was little to see except the Korper Gallery, a restoration studio, and an empty space called the Morrow Gallery that she rented to other dealers for one-time shows. Eventually a sort of community pulled itself together. The Christopher Cutts Gallery moved in, and prospered enough to expand. More recently the Genereux Grunwald Gallery set up shop, owned by Linda Genereux; Grunwald later withdrew and it became the Genereux Gallery. In 1994 the Robert Birch Gallery moved in, making four galleries. In one of the studios Jonathan Crinion began designing furniture for Knoll and other clients. Meanwhile, the local artist population increased; there are now scores of artists and designers within a few blocks. These days, openings are as well attended as they were when Korper was downtown on Spadina Avenue. Presiding over them, Korper nourishes her status as one of the dazzling figures on the Toronto art scene. A small, intense figure with purple hair, she plays several roles at once: high-toned apostle for avant-garde art, deal-making entrepreneur, and mother-figure to the artists she shows. Those who come to her gallery – for instance, a cluster of lawyers planning to expand their firm's collection – know that Olga is part of the show, sometimes the most engaging part.

The artists she encourages were among the few who liked the location from the beginning. "My artists, without exception, loved it," Korper says. "One of them said, 'If people don't think my work is worth another ten minutes in the car, to hell with them.'" Clients weren't so enthusiastic. "They'd say, 'Of course I'm going to come out, I'll follow you anywhere, but who else will?' I had maybe forty people say that to me." Just about everyone had difficulty finding it for the first time. "I had people screaming at me from their cars – Korper, what are you doing to me!" But when they got to Morrow Avenue they found they liked being there, liked discovering it, liked telling friends about their discovery and bringing them out to show it off. Linda Genereux says: "People can't believe the construction, those gigantic beams, it's like turning back time. They want to show other people."

Art is a private obsession that demands public exposure, and an art gallery mediates between the private and the public. In one way a gallery is only a store, a place to sell objects; but it's also a delicate instrument of cultural expression, by which artists begin to inject their ideas into the common culture. Uniquely, it transforms the private act of making art and buying it into something like a public performance. Creating an art gallery can be a major contribution to culture; developing new civic space where art flourishes can be still more impressive, an audacious act of citizenship as well as commerce. By the mid-1990s, no one would call the Morrow complex a commercial success. But no one could possibly call it a failure, either.

IF KORPER'S GALLERY is easy to miss, so is much of the new public art in Toronto. If you stroll down the west side of Spadina Road, from the Baldwin steps near Casa Loma to Dupont Street, past the Neo-Georgian town houses of the Castle Hill development and under the old railway bridge, you will walk both over and under an art object, though you may not know it's there. The object is *Spadina Line,* by Brad Golden and Norman Richards, completed in the summer of 1991. It's an elusive, mysterious work, and the symbol of a new era in public art. To understand it, we need to consider its background, and its place in the history of public art.

In 1989 the city planning department held a competition to generate ideas for improving the surroundings of two forlorn railway underpasses, one of them at Spadina and Dupont. Golden and Richards won the Spadina commission and set out to make a work that would integrate the underpass with the street to the north. Like many public artists of this period, they began with the idea of animating the space by drawing attention to its history.

They are among hundreds of North American and European artists who have been quietly rewriting the rules of public art. Their work represents a generational shift and a redefinition of goals: they want to make an art of public revelation rather than personal expression. The objects they produce show no common style (*Spadina Line* doesn't look like anything else I know), but you can identify the artists by their conversation and their rhetoric. Often they announce they want to *articulate* the shape of a district, *identify* its historic meaning, *reveal* the essence of the site. Unlike most artists in this century, they frequently describe their work as a story or a narrative. Like architects, they may speak of reconnecting and reintegrating districts that have been ripped apart by big buildings and roads. *Context* has become a favourite word of theirs, as it is for many architects trained since the 1970s.

Spadina Line attempts to answer the pressing problem of making art for public spaces, a problem that has been especially obvious in Toronto in recent years. There was a time, only three decades ago, when Toronto showed little interest in decorating its buildings and streets with art. That changed in 1966 with the installation of the Henry Moore sculpture in Nathan Phillips Square. When the Moore controversy finally played itself out, the idea that public art is important was embedded in Toronto's civic consciousness. It has been a potent force ever since, with mixed, sometimes dismaying results.

IN THIS CENTURY, Toronto has not found it easy to identify and celebrate its great citizens – one of the ancient purposes of public sculpture. For evidence of this failure we need to look no farther than the street signs. Toronto has no streets named for William Osler, Frederick Banting, C. H. Best, Stephen Leacock, Marshall McLuhan, Glenn Gould, Tom Thomson, or Lawren Harris. To streets that might have been given historical names, we attach words like Bay, University, and College, words that carry an implicit message: we are a plain modest people, living in a city where nothing much has happened. A guide to Metropolitan Toronto testifies to a stunted civic imagination, particularly where it lists Cedar Avenue, Cedar Brae Boulevard, Cedarcroft Boulevard, Cedarland Drive, Cedarsprings, Cedarbrae Crescent, Cedarvale Avenue, Cedarview Drive, and Cedarwood Avenue. (Somewhere a civil servant sits at a desk, brainstorming through the long nights, planning the future location of Cedarplank Boulevard.)

Toronto has a similarly inglorious tradition in monuments, but a tradition that is harder to ignore, public sculpture being more noticeable than street names. In recent generations it has not been Toronto's habit to decide that this or that citizen demands a memorial in stone or bronze – and on the rare occasions when we have made that decision, the results have usually been lamentable. After the death in 1955 of Robert H. Saunders, a famous mayor and Ontario Hydro chairman, a committee raised money for a granite monument by Emanuel Hahn, to be placed on University Avenue at College Street. It turned out to be a half-hearted gesture, embodying only a hint of the intensity and vigor of the public life it was supposed to commemorate.

Partly as a result of failures like the Saunders monument, Toronto abandoned the practice of commissioning monuments, but retained an old habit of casually accumulating them. In public art, Toronto has followed a practice no one could call a policy. Monuments appear among us unbidden, as if by accident, and polite gratitude is our only consistent principle: usually we are incapable of refusing delivery of a gift, no matter how inappropriate. The existence in Toronto of a public monument in someone's honour depends on isolated passions and whims. Toronto has no monument to Shakespeare, for instance, but we have one to Robert Burns. That's because in 1902 the Burns Literary Society erected a charming statue of him, embellished with quotations from his poetry, in Allan Gardens. There's no sign of Beethoven or Mozart in our parks, but Sibelius is there: in 1959 Finnish Canadians put up a monument to him in Jean Sibelius Square at Brunswick and Bernard Avenues. In 1975 the women's council of the Ukrainian Canadian Committee erected a statue in High Park of the poet Lesya Ukrainka, on the centennial of her birth; Dante, Shelley, and Pushkin still await local recognition. In 1977 Henry R. Jackman donated the statue of Winston Churchill on the edge of Nathan Phillips Square, but so far it has occurred to no one that another figure from the same period, Franklin Roosevelt, might deserve a similar honour.

In the early 1980s the Chinese Canadian Committee held a competition for a monument in a public park to Sun Yat-Sen, the founder of modern China. A model made by Joe Rosenthal won, but the city's advisory committee on art rejected it on grounds of quality. Meetings were held and angry letters written; Avrom Isaacs, the eminent art dealer, appeared before a city council committee to urge that it not be accepted. In February, 1984, a letter from Thomas Sun of the Chinese Canadian Committee arrived at City Hall, illustrating the pressures and tensions involved in a project of this kind. Like most such letters, it claimed intimate knowledge of the views of a vast and disparate population: "The Ethnic Chinese Community at large in Toronto wants a sculpture that they can then be proud of and identify with, and they are ecstatic with the excellent work of Mr. Joe Rosenthal." He said that, unlike monuments which seek to provoke and shock, this work "radiates the strength of Dr. Sun Yat-Sen, marching against the wind, leading the great revolution." Shortly after receiving that letter, city council set its committee's report aside and accepted the sculpture, which now stands in Riverdale Park.

One of the oddest results of our insouciant, come-what-may attitude is the monument to Robert Raikes, the English newspaper publisher who invented the Sunday school in the eighteenth century. It stands on the west side of Queen's Park Crescent, and for about forty years I've been walking past it, occasionally wondering why a memorial to someone almost never mentioned in Toronto occupies such a prominent place. The answer is that the International Council of Religious Education met in Toronto in 1930, 150 years after Raikes opened his first school in Gloucester. It seemed a good idea to commemorate that sesquicentennial by erecting a replica of the Thomas Brock monument to Raikes in London. The treasurer of the education council that year happened to be a former Canadian, J. L. Kraft, the great Chicago cheese baron, who put up the money and apparently insisted it go in Queen's Park rather than in Allan Gardens, the city's preference. So a series of accidents left us with this peculiar but not disagreeable legacy.

The statue of Raikes inspired a scene in *The Cunning Man*, the 1994 Robertson Davies novel which charts Toronto's progress from provincialism to sophistication. In the 1930s the novel's characters are restless with their lives in dour Toronto, ambitious to move beyond it and place themselves in a larger world. Davies encapsulates their attitudes in an elaborate prank focused on the Raikes monument.

The narrator-hero, Dr. Jonathan Hullah, studying at the University of Toronto, comes under the sway of one Darcy Dwyer, a man who views the pretensions of Methodist Toronto with ironic disdain. Dwyer believes that actors are insufficiently memorialized by modern society, and organizes an ingenious remedy. He notes that the "wigged and ruffled" Raikes depicted by the sculptor has a graceful, imposing look. He decides this could be a depiction of David Garrick: "The pose, pointing at the book – mightn't it be his copy of *Hamlet?*" Darcy hires a man to make a new plaque for the plinth. One night, after midnight, Dwyer and Hullah go to Queen's Park for a secret installation. A monument maker arrives with the new plaque, bores holes, and expertly fixes his creation on the statue, "a job of exquisite craftsmanship." Dwyer then strips a sheet of paper away and reveals the new inscription:

DAVID GARRICK 1717-1779
I am disappointed by that stroke of death which has eclipsed the gaiety of nations and impoverished the public stock of harmless pleasure – Dr. Samuel Johnson. Erected by lovers of the Player's Art.

For $450, plus tip, Dwyer has redesignated the statue. "Now let's get the hell out of here before the police arrive," he says. But, the narrator tells us, "no police arrived then or for long after, so far as I know. Which raises the question: Who looks at inscriptions on public statuary?" Certainly those who read *The Cunning Man* will check the Raikes inscription.

If future Torontonians are puzzled by the statue of Raikes, they may be astounded by the *Canadian Airmen's Memorial,* by Oscar Nemon, at University Avenue and Dundas Street – a spectacularly bad work on a spectacularly good site, a large, permanent speck in the eye of the city. It was a gift from the Jackman Foundation, which the city felt compelled to accept. The work is not just bad, it's insistently bad; if there is an artist anywhere in Toronto who admires it, that artist has remained silent. Worse, it dominates a busy corner of the main boulevard; unlike many unfortunate gifts to the city, it cannot be ignored. The day in 1984 when the Queen unveiled it was the low point in the history of public sculpture in Toronto.

There's no use in protesting, of course. The Nemon will not disappear in the imaginable future: an unwritten but unbreakable rule holds that we never dismantle a public monument that commemorates war service. But that mistake can never be far from the minds of those who run Toronto's public art program and the Public Art Commission, a city-appointed body of experts that provides advice on art for public land or art provided by developers in exchange for concessions on land use. *Canadian Airmen's Memorial* performs the role played by the skull that medieval scholars kept on their desks to remind them of their mortality. It's an always-present example of how badly things can go wrong.

Jane Perdue, a City Hall art administrator, wasn't speaking of Nemon's work when she reflected on our history one day in 1993, but she might well have been. "We end up with art in the public realm and wonder how it got there," she said. "Usually it got there because a few people thought it should be there." That isn't good enough, obviously, but neither is the idea of a czar at City Hall arbitrarily accepting or rejecting private offerings. So the city has set up a system of consultants and jurors who work with developers and donors. People who want to commission art are now told how to hire a consultant and set up a competition. In the end, city council must accept responsibility for the results. Some of us may continue to regard specific art objects as deplorable, but the system provides a degree of legitimacy. As Perdue says, "Because art is subjective, there has to be a credible process so that the council can say: This is how it worked."

WHEN IT WORKS, a public art object installs itself permanently in our collective imagination. That's certainly the case with Derek Michael Besant's mural on the Flatiron Building. When it appeared over Front Street in 1980, looking like a clipping torn from a magazine and carelessly pinned to a wall, it seemed flimsy and temporary. To many people strolling past the St. Lawrence Centre it was a mere visual pun, a painting of a painting that incorporated both "real" and "unreal" windows. Since our culture classifies humour as trivial, the work's subtle wit made it easy to dismiss. An art director friend told me at the time, "It's a single joke – you'll tire of it by next year." But we didn't tire of it. In the 1980s and 1990s, nearly every book about Toronto included a photograph of it; the great Hungarian photographer André Kertész took a picture that wound up in one of his books. After ten years it was a famous Toronto landmark in its own right, and today painting over it might well arouse as much fury as destroying the 1882 building it adorns.

Besant's work was a success because he made Berczy Park more distinctive than it would have been otherwise (the literal purpose of a "landmark"), because he made his mural complex enough to invite repeated examination, because he expressed the ironic and ambivalent tone of his own historic period, and because he connected his work to its immediate environment by echoing the brickwork of the old buildings nearby.

A success like the Flatiron mural seems, in retrospect, a small miracle. It emerged from a long process of selection and coordination, a process that would seem designed to grind an art object into mediocrity. It was in part the gift of A. E. LePage Real Estate, Royal Insurance, and the Lavalin corporation, which were all involved in developing Front Street East. It had to be approved not only by city politicians and bureaucrats but also (because it was on a historic building) by the Toronto Historical Board and the Ontario Heritage Foundation.

A committee of seven, including curators, an artist, a developer, and a town planner first decided who could compete for the commission. The committee chose six artists, who submitted proposals in sketch form to a final jury, which chose Besant's design. The project cost the three sponsoring corporations $40,000, which was matched by an Ontario government grant from lottery proceeds. Besant received $8,000 and a permanent place in the cityscape of Toronto.

The process of approval can also produce failures, and sometimes the best we can say for them is that they are a little more interesting than *Canadian Airmen's Memorial* or another piece that was accepted by the politicians over the objections of their art committee – Francesco Pirelli's *Monument to Multiculturalism,* the clumsy exercise in sentimental symbolism that stands outside Union Station, a gift from the National Congress of Italian-Canadians. Another failure of the approval process is the collection of sculptures designed by Eldon Garnet for police headquarters on College Street; their plonking literalness (a policewoman illustrates the building of our future by constructing, trowel in hand, a granite pyramid) makes them bad in a peculiarly post-modern way, and their location on the sidewalk makes them painfully unavoidable.

On the sidewalk at the northwest corner of Yonge and Bloor Streets, another sculpture, a flamboyant bronze clock, is the end result of a sculpture competition that nearly went wrong. This elaborate folly by the American artist Wendell Castle may not be a great moment in the history of sculpture (it suggests modish Italian furniture of the 1980s), but as public art it works well. It punctuates the corner, as a landmark should. It neatly reflects its environment by embodying both the trashy glitz of Yonge Street and the chic of Bloor. And in 1988 it undoubtedly added value to the 2 Bloor Street West building, whose owners, Hammerson Canada, paid $125,000 for it.

The history of Castle's clock illustrates the dangers awaiting those who stray into the world of public art, and suggests how they may sometimes be avoided. The original idea, developed by the company and its art consultant, Jeanne Parkin, was for a major piece of sculpture, probably by an artist of international reputation. Parkin set up a committee that included curators from Boston, Vancouver, and Montreal, as well as Toronto, and the committee invited several sculptors to submit proposals.

That's when trouble loomed. The head of Hammerson Canada, Bruce Heyland, looked at some earlier sculptures by the artists chosen and didn't like any of them. Parkin knew this had happened before, with another Hammerson building at 70 University Avenue. On that occasion, the choice had slipped away from the experts and into the hands of company executives. The result is *Pas de Trois*, a lamentable piece in stainless steel by Russell Jacques, that looks like a squashed treble clef. I have never heard a kind word said about it.

Hammerson appeared headed for another disaster, and Parkin decided to avoid it. "Rather than asking for maquettes," she said later, "I simply aborted the competition right there." Instead, she got in touch with Castle, an artist she admired who wasn't on the committee's list. In six months, Castle came up with a design that both Parkin and Heyland liked.

EVEN IF THE PROCESS of approval is sorted out, a difficult question remains: Once expert advisors are chosen, what principles should they follow? Through most of history, public art has been erected to the glory of God, the empire, or the state. In Toronto today, none of those purposes has broad public appeal, and no clear alternative presents itself. *The Art of the Avenue*, a 1989 Metro Toronto planning department report on sculpture for University Avenue, notes that before the Second World War, public art was normally made with public consent – monuments could often "successfully focus broadly-held community values supported by an acceptable level of taste." But after 1945, the new public sculpture on University Avenue was no more than architectural embellishment. The town planners who wrote the report acknowledged the reason: there is no evidence that "a basis for such consent exists in the pluralistic society that has evolved in Toronto since the Second World War." Most of the recent public art illustrates a shift "from a broadly-based, consensual activity towards a personal, self-interest activity." On University Avenue, these "essentially personal and often private statements" have eroded the stature of the street as a symbolic centre of Metropolitan Toronto.

Sculpture can work purely as a decorative landmark that distinguishes one street corner from another, a useful function when so many buildings look like so many others; but shouldn't it also have coherent purpose? Shouldn't it say something? One obvious function of public art is to bring into the open the talents of certain artists whose work is otherwise available mainly in galleries and museums. Kosso Eloul and Sorel Etrog, the two sculptors who have received the most public commissions, fit this category. Kosso has sixteen sculptures on display around Toronto, the most prominent at the corner of Church and Bloor Streets; Etrog has a dozen, including the gigantic hand commissioned by Olympia and York for the southwest corner of King and York Streets. Michael Snow has made three prominent public sculptures: the lovely Canada Geese flying through the Eaton Centre, the grotesque figures that decorate the SkyDome, and the metal tree at the corner of Jarvis and Bloor. In each case the artists fit the sculpture to the site, but their art contains no specifically public message; whether good or bad, most of this work could be placed with equal effect almost anywhere else (an exception is the SkyDome sculpture). It doesn't offer any local relevance. It's more or less the sort of work they show in art galleries, on a grander scale.

The new public art, sometimes called "contextualist," finds a sense of purpose in a reverence for place, community, and history. By evoking the history of a site, contextualist art tries to give tangible form to human memory. In Canada the best example is the collection of ten large sculptures by Melvin Charney in the garden of the Canadian Centre for Architecture in Montreal. Each of them refers both to architectural history and to the history of Montreal, and a series of plates in the wall of the garden directs us to buildings that are visible on the Montreal skyline. The Charney pieces enhance the city around them by focusing our attention on its history. In Charney's hands, sculpture preaches attentiveness to architecture as a civic virtue.

Nothing so ambitious has been projected for Toronto, but a long-range plan for public art, developed under the city planning commissioner, Robert E. Millward, rests on similar assumptions. The department surveyed the city to identify places where art can enhance the surroundings and create a sense of identity. The redevelopment of the Lower Don Valley, for instance, will create an ideal site for environmental art.

An elaborate plan for the inner harbour demonstrates how long-range planning may work. When outlining a competition for a $750,000 work of art to be placed in the new Harbour Square Park beside the ferry docks (paid for by Graywood Developments), the city decided to consider the entire inner harbour. It called for designs that could be done in stages: first the work for Harbour Square Park, later three more major works, connected in style and theme, to be placed on the Island and at the Eastern and Western Gaps. T-Zero Design, which consists of two recent architectural graduates from the University of Waterloo, Paul DeFigueiredo and Jonathan Fung, won the commission. Their large piece for Harbour Square, which includes a sundial, a fountain, a pool, and a plaza, was installed in 1995. Their related works (involving a water clock, a wind tower, and a sextant) will be made only when and if money becomes available. The four-part, harbour-spanning work might take thirty or forty years to complete; but if all goes well, these landmark-size representations of traditional ways to measure the elements will emphasize the meaning and tradition of the harbour.

The same sort of thinking produced *Spadina Line*. Brad Golden and Norman Richards started out with the idea of suggesting how much history their site contains, but the piece they made isn't obviously didactic. Their goal was to work their ideas into the fabric of the site and insinuate historic memory into public consciousness. They erected a series of sculptured lamp posts whose lights shine in circles onto the sidewalk; and in the sidewalk they inserted seven capitalized words in bronze: IRO-QUOIS, FURROW, SURVEY, AVENUE, POWER, DAIRY, and ARCHIVE. Iroquois refers to the prehistoric Lake Iroquois which began here and covered much of what is now downtown Toronto, Furrow refers to the market gardens that were here a century ago, Survey acknowledges the laying out of Toronto in the late eighteenth century, and so on; the last word in the series, Archive, welcomes the latest user of the site, the Metropolitan Toronto Archives building on the other side of Spadina.

Is *Spadina Line* a success? Certainly it causes talk. From time to time people can be heard asking each other what it means and discussing its implications, which satisfies one of the purposes of this kind of art. A major oversight is the lack of any explanation or artists' signatures, which will eventually be rectified by a plaque. One of the admirers of the work is June Ardiel, who spent four years preparing an illustrated catalogue, *Sculpture Toronto*, published in 1994. She thinks it works superbly, even if only for a minority. "For most people, it doesn't exist. It's very peripheral to their vision. But for those who see it, it's beautiful and elegant. It adds another dimension to the street and unifies it." I've been walking through it for a couple of years, examining it from every angle, and I'm still not sure it's entirely successful. All I know for certain is that it makes this corner of Toronto more interesting, and makes the future of public sculpture look wonderfully promising.

13

The CBC's Awkward Palace

THE FUTURE SEEMED relatively promising for the Canadian Broadcasting Corporation in the 1970s, when its managers set out to buy some land for a Toronto headquarters. A new building was badly needed. Since the 1950s, CBC Toronto had been living in a dispersed slum, some two dozen different locations across the city, most of them ramshackle. Acquiring a piece of property was the first step toward bringing all this activity under one roof. In 1978 the corporation paid $19.3 million for 9.3 acres on John Street, between Front and Wellington Streets. That was a large expenditure, but nine years later it looked modest. The CBC had placed its bet on the westward development of Toronto, and won. In 1987 a developer calculated that the property was worth about $160 million.

An increase in an asset's value naturally pleases those who acquired it, but this particular windfall turned out to be a misfortune. It drew the CBC into a transaction that was hideously inappropriate and produced a building that is altogether wrong. It also linked Toronto, by a circuitous route, to one of the most bizarre figures in all of modern architecture.

A generation ago, in *Parkinson's Law,* the economic historian C. Northcote Parkinson argued that every great institution begins to decline as soon as it moves into a gleaming new building. No reader of Parkinson could fail to notice that as the CBC grew less significant, its Toronto building grew more ambitious. When it finally opened, in 1993, the scale was wildly out of proportion to the CBC's activities and audiences. It was the grandest broadcasting centre anyone in Canada ever imagined, but it produces fewer programs than the CBC created many years ago in cramped, threadbare buildings on Jarvis Street.

What made the project especially questionable was the CBC's decision to play at real estate as well as broadcasting. In the early 1980s, the CBC concluded that it would be foolish to use this precious site merely for its own purposes. The idea of a big property development was raised. A private developer would be brought in and a commercial development as well as a broadcast centre would be built: an office tower, stores, a hotel, 4 million square feet in all. The CBC would then rent space from the developer and end up owning its building.

Having acquired its own momentum, the planning continued even as the fortunes of the corporation declined. CBC executives, faced with a tighter budget every year, were closing facilities elsewhere and cutting staff, but nothing stopped the Broadcasting Centre. It had developed a crazy internal logic. In 1986, even Brian Mulroney's federal government – which otherwise looked with scorn on the CBC – acknowledged that the Broadcasting Centre was inevitable. The responsible deputy minister in Ottawa said that the building itself would in the end cost nothing. He acknowledged that equipping it would run to about $300 million, but that could be seen as an industrial subsidy for the electronics industry.

This was nonsense, but precisely the kind of nonsense that politicians and bureaucrats – not to mention a few capitalists – accept as truth. The CBC, and the government to which it reported, had fallen victim to a warped idea that has afflicted the arts across Canada, a belief that a cultural building has a value separate from what it contains. This pathology – long ago given the name "edifice complex" – took root in the run-up to the Canadian centennial in 1967 and turned out to be a habit Canada couldn't shake. Employment is one reason. When a potential concert hall is discussed with government, it's rated according to how many thousands of work days it will provide for the building trades. Prestige is another. Concert halls and art galleries produce pleasant headlines and newspaper photos of cabinet ministers delivering checks and cutting ribbons. Meanwhile, artists live in poverty and arts institutions have trouble paying the bills for everyday activities. In the arts, including broadcasting, a perverse rule applies: capital investment is inherently good, operating expenses inherently bad.

In 1987 Cadillac Fairview won the competition to develop the CBC's property. By the time the decision was made, the company had been sold to Chicago interests. So the most expensive cultural agency of the Canadian government found itself in partnership with an American corporation, an arrangement its directors and supporters would hardly have chosen. Stranger still, Cadillac Fairview had decided that the architect would be Philip Johnson. The CBC, after steadfastly refusing to run its networks on a star system, found itself involved with a building designed by the greatest architectural star of the age.

Canadian architects were, naturally, upset. Arthur Erickson wrote to the president of the CBC to say that the use of an American was an insult to Canadian architects. In his view, CBC headquarters required a sensitive understanding of Canada, which presumably no American could possess. Boris Zerafa, a Toronto architect, went further: "I don't think in any other country you'd find a foreign architect building a major cultural project like this." He must have forgotten Paris, where most of the major cultural projects built or planned in the last generation have gone to foreign architects – the Pompidou Centre (an Englishman and an Italian), the Bastille opera house (a Canadian), the Louvre extension (an American), and the Musée d'Orsay (an Italian). Arguably, all of these projects were more important national monuments than a property development wrapped around a broadcasting facility.

Still, Johnson was an odd choice. He was not just an American architect but *the* American architect, the favourite of big developers from Boston to San Francisco. How he reached that point is one of the fascinating stories of modern culture.

AT THE MUSEUM of Modern Art in New York in 1932, Johnson was one of two organizers of the most influential architectural exhibit in history, the show that first preached the gospel of modernism in the United States and installed the phrase "International Style" in the language. From then until the 1970s, he was the most articulate and energetic partisan of modernism in the world. At the MOMA – with which he's been associated for more than half a century – Johnson organized exhibitions that promoted Ludwig Mies van der Rohe and his followers as the only important architects and their style as the only one appropriate for this century. Johnson helped bring Mies to America from Germany in 1937, and after completing his own architectural education – he went back to Harvard and took his degree at the age of thirty-seven – worked joyfully in Mies's shadow. His own house, in New Canaan, Connecticut, designed under Mies's influence, is a modernist classic. In 1958 Johnson worked with his master on the Seagram building in New York, one of the great events in Mies's career.

But at some point in the 1960s the International Style began to look tired, and after Mies's death in 1969 it became obvious that the buildings of his followers were rigid and boring. Architects described as "post-modernist" began to reassert the value of ornament and historical styles. That was exactly what Johnson had campaigned against in the 1930s, when he put non-Miesian architects on the defensive by ridiculing the old Beaux-Arts style. But now, amazingly, Johnson adjusted. In fact, he did more than adjust. First he became the friend of the post-modernists, then he turned out to be the most prominent post-modernist himself. It was as if the czar's son had come out of the palace and taken over leadership of the Bolsheviks.

At a convention of architects in Dallas in 1978, Johnson said: "We are at a watershed, at the end of modernism as we have known it.... We don't want everything to look like a glass box any more." Whether he said who had championed all those glass boxes in the first place is not recorded. The man who had taught Americans the hard, cold rules of modern architecture – and had helped turn modernism into a crusade as well as a style – was now teaching the opposite. But his conversion did not produce the derisive laughter that might have been expected. To the contrary: his new approach proved more profitable than his old. While he acknowledged that the switch in attitudes was "almost embarrassing," potential clients did not share his unease. They liked him better than other post-modernists, perhaps because he combined the authority of the old (that is, modernism) with the freshness of the new. While younger post-modernists spent much of their time designing houses and other minor buildings, Johnson scooped up the major commissions. He even designed a cathedral, a California television evangelist's $18-million glass building, whose opening in 1980 was sardonically described by *The New York Times* as "probably the most exciting event in Orange County since the completion of Disneyland." The evangelist was impressed by the piety the architect showed while applying for the commission. Later Johnson said, "I wanted to do the job. I got religious."

Most important, Johnson designed the AT&T building in New York, on whose top he placed a thirty-foot-high Chippendale-style ornamental cutout. The opening of that building in 1984 was a climactic moment of post-modernism, as well as the final recantation of Johnson's old views. "If Mies van der Rohe were alive today," wrote a critic in the Chicago *Tribune,* "he would regard this design with loathing." There was no reason to think that such comments bothered Johnson. He had developed a public style that uniquely mixed insouciance and cynicism. In 1982, at the University of Virginia, he was asked what principles lay behind his plan for a new building in Boston. He replied, "I do not believe in principles.... I am a whore, and I am paid very well for building high-rise buildings."

Whore is a word not often used by architectural critics, but Johnson's eagerness to please attracted hostility. His work of the last fifteen years owes more to showmanship than to architecture; its flashiness suggests stage sets rather than buildings. Having abandoned the rules he learned in his youth, Johnson learned no others to replace them. The result, most of the time, was pointlessness and emptiness. The architectural critic Diana Ketcham wrote: "The lesson of Johnson's first forty years in architecture is that he performs brilliantly as a promoter of others' talent, and respectably as an imitator of that talent. The lesson of his last, prolific decade is that he performs execrably when freed to be himself." Despite what the Canadian architects said, Johnson's nationality was the least of his drawbacks.

All this was known when Johnson was embraced by the CBC. But there was another problem, which the Canadians could not have understood: just as the CBC became Johnson's client, he was entering a troubled phase in his career. About the time the building got under way, Johnson and his partner, John Burgee, were discovering cracks in their partnership. The younger Burgee was trying to establish a reputation that would outlast the death of Johnson, who was born in 1906. First Burgee added his name at the top of the letterhead beside Johnson's; later he managed to demote Johnson from partner to design consultant. Meanwhile, he explained to anyone who would listen that these weren't just Johnson buildings and that he, Burgee, had a lot to do with designing them. The relationship between the two partners was further strained when the recession made commissions scarce. Well before CBC employees began moving into their new home, Burgee and Johnson publicly and acrimoniously divorced. "I feel he threw me out," Johnson told a *Wall Street Journal* reporter. "The problem was his own sense of defeat." Around the same time, the firm sought protection from its creditors in bankruptcy court.

Still, these problems don't explain the mess that Johnson and Burgee made of the CBC building's exteriors. They applied the word "deconstructivist" to their design, and a year after it opened Johnson explained to a Toronto *Star* critic: "It is slightly deconstructivist; I designed it while I was curating the deconstructivist show at the Museum of Modern Art." That exhibition was an attempt to import into architecture the deconstructivist literary theories that had been dominating English studies for years.

In architecture, deconstructivism apparently meant calling into question the ordinary assumptions of building: whereas traditional architecture tries to look solid and permanent, a deconstructivist building might look as if it were about to fall down. Perhaps the studios placed on the CBC roof were in that category – they looked like building blocks haphazardly strewn about by a child. Elsewhere, the design turned out to be unremarkable. The peculiar style of the facades amounts to no more than a banal elaboration on familiar modernist grids: a lot of gray lines and red crosses drawn for no apparent purpose on the sides of a warehouse built to ungainly proportions. Watching the building come together over about two years, I kept wondering when the finish would be applied and some sort of aesthetic sense would emerge. It never happened.

The CBC building is one work of art that seems even worse after its creators explain their purposes. John Burgee on the facades: "We created a very bright red secondary grid as a fine line that penetrated behind the super grid to further break down the scale and mass of the building, thus making it more human." Burgee and Johnson didn't choose that colour all by themselves. They brought in a consultant, Donald Kaufman, of Kaufman Color, who explained: "The red on the secondary grid strikes an important note. Red is the colour...of very high definition and intensity." Thank you. As for Johnson himself, he was pleased with his achievement. The Broadcasting Centre, he told a Toronto journalist, is "by far the most interesting building of mine, the most daring." There is no building in the world so bad that its architect won't tell you it's great; but even by the standards of architectural egomania, Johnson went too far.

THE BARBARA FRUM ATRIUM of the CBC is named for a great broadcaster who in her private life was both an imaginative gardener and a sensitive patron of architecture. That gives the name a heavy charge of irony, since the atrium remains curiously barren of planting and its architectural style is monumentally simple-minded. Still, it honestly states the true nature of the building it introduces. A heavy-handed attempt to create charm with blatant toy-store colours, like the screaming green of the gigantic elevator shaft, announces the aesthetic failure at the core of the enterprise, and a visitor will later find little to soften this first impression. More important, the emptiness of the atrium symbolizes the disappointed hopes and misplaced priorities that left Toronto and the CBC with an unlovely and impractical building.

The atrium turns out to be much larger than photographs or numbers (10,000 square feet, ten storeys high) can convey – and yet it has little reason to be there. Normally, an office-building atrium throws natural light onto interior offices, but in this case the offices are mostly hidden behind blank walls: the light falls pointlessly onto a vast, multicoloured terrazzo floor. The CBC's atrium spectacularly illustrates the most often quoted principle of modern design, form follows function, but in reverse. Here we have plenty of form, but no function.

The architects aren't idiots; they didn't plan it this way. They designed interior windows, so that many employees who are not important enough to have outside offices would look onto the atrium – a nice second prize. Along the way, when the budget had to be cut, someone pointed out that windows cost more than walls. So most of the windows were eliminated and most of the atrium's meaning disappeared. It's now used for occasional public events, like carolers singing in Christmas week, and for some big CBC functions. A few concerts have been recorded there, and musicians have found the space acoustically rich and stimulating. Otherwise, it lacks purpose.

The same gigantic scale that created the embarrassment of the atrium also produced a nightmare of confusion in the design of the interior. The building is dedicated to the art of communications, but it can't begin to communicate its own shape to the people who work there or visit. It's a cumbersome, helpless giant. When you examine the floor plans, you understand that at some point this project went wildly out of control. The designers of the interior faced two major problems. Each floor covers three and a half acres, a huge space to manage, and the structure (being built around the atrium) made it impossible to arrange the offices and studios in street-like patterns. So the designers instead divided each floor into nine lettered sections, with numbering inside each section: if an office's address is 3C209, it's on the third floor, in C section.

On paper it seemed coherent, but when built the Broadcasting Centre turned into a source of comedy. For weeks after moving in, people spent much of their time exchanging stories about trying to get from one office to another. One afternoon, walking the halls, I overheard seven snatches of conversation; five were about the problem of finding directions. I encountered a young man talking to himself. "Now where am I going?" he asked. (A radio attached to his belt indicated he was a security guard.) A week or so after moving in, the host of *As It Happens,* Michael Enright, couldn't find the way back to his office from the cafeteria. Every time he turned a promising corner, he confronted a blank wall. Finally he took the nearest elevator to the street door, pretended he was arriving for work, and started again. "You can't improvise," he explained later. "It's unforgiving. There's one way to go, and if you don't go that way you're lost."

The building management tried to help by installing forty video terminals, called "search centres," near the elevators. The process of using them started playfully, like a display at the Ontario Science Centre. A recorded voice spoke, and a musical phrase played. You typed in the name of the person or department you wanted and a map appeared, with one pulsing light to show where you were and another to show where you wanted to go. An excellent idea, but on the screen the floor plan looked like electronic circuitry: it was the sort of map that could be read only by someone who already knew the way. When I was visiting a radio executive, I managed to get as far as the correct corner of the correct floor. Knowing I could be no more than four or five offices from my quarry, I turned to the video terminal to find the way. As on previous occasions, I found it unreadable, but I made a wild guess at what it was saying – and then headed off in precisely the wrong direction. I wandered through a maze of corridors, all of them looking exactly the same. It was like being lost in Algonquin Park. ("Didn't we pass that tree two hours ago?") In practice, the video terminals' main function was to amuse staff members with the spectacle of visitors trying to use them. Still, if you stood long enough in front of one, and cursed a bit as you pressed the buttons, someone would come along and help. In the summer of 1995 a budget cut provided an excuse to shut down the whole system.

These are relatively minor annoyances when set beside the cultural problem built into the centre. Broadcasters, particularly public broadcasters, intensely dislike uniformity and formality. They like variety and surprise. Many of them wear jeans and sweatshirts to work, and sometimes their offices are as messy as college dorms. On John Street the employees may appreciate the much improved studio facilities and the fact that all CBC departments are in one place, rather than scattered around the city. But the match between people and environment doesn't work, and many who use the building appear to feel severe discomfort. It's as if the entire University of Toronto faculty, with all its support staff, were moved into the T-D Centre. One evidence of uneasiness is the raging paranoia that appeared among the staff in the early weeks, producing a wave of rumours: the lighting damages your eyes, the electronic security-check entrances secretly monitor attendance, there's a weapons room in the basement in case of civil disturbance, and (my favourite) there's one toilet in the building to be used only by the Queen.

In the early days you could read the signs of tension in *Up Front,* a chatty little in-house newspaper. One issue noted that some employees, accustomed to being able to open office windows, were not happy with a sealed, climate-controlled building. *Up Front's* editors solved this problem by telling their readers that city air isn't good for them anyway: "Just how fresh is the air we desperately seek by opening a window? Studies have proven outdoor air in an urban setting can no longer be considered fresh...." There are people who can accept that sort of misguided paternalism without anger, but they tend not to work at the CBC.

The contrast between the financial status of the corporation and the appearance of its new home is equally glaring. The CBC, owned by the taxpayers, is living in what looks like a corporate palace. After pleading poor for as long as anybody can remember, it suddenly moved into a setting that speaks eloquently of prosperity – and that tone continued to dominate the design of the contents.

A year or so after most of the building was occupied, studios were designed for the news programs. I went down to see them, and discovered a remarkable fact: during off-air hours, a yellow foam-rubber cushion is wrapped around the edges of the glass top of the desk from which Peter Mansbridge reads the evening news. It took me a while to find out its purpose: low-tech protection against a high-tech hazard. During rehearsal, the padding protects the desk from rogue robocameras. In this studio, old-fashioned camera operators have been replaced by a single technician whose computer controls the movement of four cameras. Occasionally a robocamera goes wonky and starts crashing blindly around the room, endangering expensive furniture. Sometimes, if a camera runs amok, the operator jumps up and pursues it, like a zookeeper chasing a baby elephant.

This is a minor problem encountered by the people responsible for the news studios. A team of in-house designers headed by Roy Kellar was assigned to create a style for the news that comes out of Toronto and several other cities. The idea was to give viewers "a visual cue" that they were watching the CBC. The project was part of the "repositioning strategy," an attempt to make the CBC stand out among the increasing number of channels. Moving the major newscast from 10 P.M. to 9 P.M., a key element in repositioning, was declared a failure even before new studios were finished. The news then moved back to the old time, but the new design strategy went ahead anyway.

The Mansbridge desk itself – more than thirteen feet across, more than six feet deep – symbolizes the style. It has a lavish, money-is-no-object look. Derek Fenske, who designed it, dealt ingeniously with the problem of discreetly satisfying Mansbridge's needs. Beneath the glass top, Fenske buried six television monitors and a computer screen, and he built into various hidden nooks an array of other objects: a pullout computer keyboard, a phone with many lines, and a trough for carrying cables. He put green leather trim on the inner edges of the glass top, to muffle the noise of hands or jewelry. He designed the desk for use by either one or two anchors. Some distance away, the designers built a separate set to be used by the host of *Prime Time Magazine.*

People accustomed to visiting television studios were astonished by these new studios. Many years ago, when I first appeared on television, I was surprised by the ramshackle quality of the studio. On the screen at home, *Fighting Words,* a panel show, seemed to take place in sleek, glamorous "Danish modern" surroundings. When I got there I discovered that everything seemed to be made of plywood, poorly banged together; the chairs were standard cafeteria issue. That, of course, was show business. Anyone involved in theatre or films makes the same sort of discovery: things aren't as they appear.

The same principle works at the CBC, but backwards. On my home screen, the CBC news does not make a strong visual impression. Except for the unusual depth of the main cover shot of Mansbridge, it looks much like other news shows. But when you see and touch the real thing, it turns out to be better than it appears on screen. A small round table behind Mansbridge's desk, like the pillars and other curving surfaces in the room, is finished in bands of light ash, expertly applied. The maps on the walls aren't temporary sketches on cheap plastic: they are literally etched into half-inch sandblasted glass. The wall surface that works like a scrim in the theatre (depending on the lighting, it looks either solid or transparent) isn't gauze but well-made metal mesh. The standard furniture is good-quality Steelcase and Teknion. The sets have an unexpectedly permanent feeling. As Kellar says, "It's part interior architecture, part set."

Since the first years of CNN, in the early 1980s, the standard format for television news has included a shot of writers and producers working at their terminals in a newsroom. In fifteen years, the public status of news editors has radically changed: where once they worked entirely in private, they are now glimpsed at their desks by hundreds of millions of people every day. Kellar says the news department wanted that brisk, busy look to give viewers "a feeling of authenticity." According to

Bob Conroy, the director of production for television news and current affairs, "We believe it adds a credibility to the service."

This format is now so popular that on some European networks, where the newsroom and the studios are in different places, the producers fake it by having the news read against a chroma-key shot of people at terminals. The British Broadcasting Corporation international service looks unusual because it eliminates the newsroom and places the announcer against a blue background which appears to be a studio flat but is in fact a blank television picture. The CBC newsroom, needless to say, is no fake. People seen in the large room where Mansbridge works are actual editors actually preparing programs, or at least looking busy.

Every design carries a message, but the message of these studios is baffling – as baffling as the building in which they're housed. Apparently poverty-stricken, the CBC constructed lavish facilities for its news service and other divisions – facilities that made little or no difference to the programs sent out to the viewers. How could that happen? How, in fact, could the building itself happen? The luck of the draw has a shaping force in any major architectural project. On this occasion the CBC's luck, and Toronto's, was mostly bad.

14

The Accidental Masterpiece

THE MOST STRIKING recent example of the role played by accident in making the new Toronto is the Bay-Adelaide Centre, the gigantic land development that will someday, God willing, spread north from Adelaide Street between Bay and Yonge. As it unfolded, the story of Bay-Adelaide turned into a revealing public comedy. It made surprised victims out of some powerful businessmen, including Ken Thomson and Edward and Peter Bronfman, and it gave the city government a peculiar victory in a contest it was widely believed to have lost.

There's a paradox behind recent Toronto development. David Lewis Stein of the *Star* addressed it, in tones of wonderment, in a 1992 column. Stein loves the way the city's downtown has evolved but understands that it could have happened only through a series of actions that, individually, were mistakes. "Prudent businessmen and responsible politicians could never have created anything like the new downtown," he wrote. "Only in a time of near madness could something like all this come together. But our grandchildren will thank us for it and marvel that we had such foresight."

Stein wasn't talking about Bay-Adelaide Park, but it helps illustrate his point. This story begins long, long ago – in the 1980s, a period so unlike the present that it seems as distant as the Second World War. In the 1980s people thought in different ways, talked a different language, and worked from radically

different assumptions. Otherwise sane capitalists fought ferociously for the right to build office towers, in the belief that the
number of tenants willing to rent space would increase indefinitely. Bankers, also presumably sane, eagerly lent money to the
tower-builders, which encouraged more people to build towers.
They were all caught up in a collective madness that seized the
business leadership of North America. Mass amnesia wiped out
all knowledge of economic cycles and past recessions. A few
executives who dared to warn that what goes up must come
down were regarded as spoilsports. James Grant, the author of
Money of the Mind, discussing these issues before a congression-
al committee in Washington, remarked, "People with money, act-
ing in crowds, periodically go off the deep end." Real estate was
Toronto's deep end in the 1980s, and the Bay-Adelaide Centre
was where Ken Thomson's Markborough Properties and the
Bronfmans' Trizec Corporation went off it, together.

Bay-Adelaide was the last great development approved by
Toronto council during the Bonus Era. While it lasted, from 1982
to 1988, the Bonus Era turned the profession of planning upside
down, called into question the most fundamental practices of city
building, and made local politics even more confusing and rancorous than it had been when the era started. At the beginning,
Toronto had an Official Plan, which dictated what kind of buildings, of which size, could be built where. City council also had
certain goals, from low-cost housing to the preservation of heritage buildings and the creation of parks. An idea grew popular
within city government: a developer who helped the city achieve
its goals would be rewarded with a bonus. City council would
allow a higher building, with more rentable office space – "a
negotiated site-specific Official Plan amendment," in plannerese.
The Ontario Planning Act makes deals of this sort legal, and for
many years cities have traded property-use concessions for open
space and other amenities. But no other Ontario municipality has
used the system so extensively as Toronto did in the 1980s.

The concessions that the city gave to Campeau Corporation's
Scotia Plaza in 1982 signaled the opening of the Bonus Era.
If Scotia Plaza could break every rule in the book, and build

about twice the space authorized by the Official Plan, then what couldn't be done by others? From that point to 1988, almost every major development in downtown Toronto received substantial space bonuses. Exceptions to the Official Plan became the rule. Every arrangement that worked its way through the bargaining process had some merit, but collectively the dealmaking raised an embarrassing question: If the Official Plan could be changed this often, what good was it? In the late 1980s, reform politics turned on this question.

WHILE PREPARING THE PLAN in 1976, planners set down certain numbers — so much density here, so much open space there — and implied that these figures had been worked out with care. If the same planners announced in 1986 that the same spaces could accommodate much more density, providing that certain concessions were made, then their new opinion cast grave doubt on the value of their old one. In truth, many planners will admit that what they do is at best an inexact science, that most Official Plan numbers are guesses, and that ten or twenty storeys added onto a forty-storey building won't make a hell of a lot of difference to anyone, provided they don't strain services like transport and sewers (none of the Bonus Era projects did).

But some citizens, and some politicians, persisted in believing that the Official Plan meant what it said. They came to think there was something underhanded in the practice of promiscuously amending it. Whatever benefits it brought, the process became unpalatable. People spoke derisively of "let's-make-a-deal planning," a phrase that embodies an unrealistic idea of what planners actually do. It seemed to imply that planners, instead of making deals, should be shaping the city in the direction of an ideal utopian form based firmly on sound principles. Since no such body of universally accepted principles exists, an official plan can never be more than the rough sketch of a desirable future.

In the Bonus Era, the role of planners changed. Once primarily the protectors of property values, they now became social planners and policy entrepreneurs, dealmakers for the public sector. Bonusing put more discretion in their hands, and made them more creative and powerful. They liked it.

A bonus system is a legal euphemism. The reality is that the public sells to developers the right to put up the sort of buildings that, theoretically, we don't want. (If we did want them, again theoretically, we wouldn't make them unlawful in the Official Plan.) In return the city receives something we believe is good. It's a form of municipal extortion, and it might be more honest if we simply demanded cash in return for every square foot of commercial space built. But that would look too much like a tax; its obviousness would make people nervous. Besides, developers would soon be trading Official Plan amendments like taxi licenses.

The central flaw in the bonus system is that it distorts community planning. Why should Toronto build 500 units of affordable housing because a developer wants to put up a tower on Wellington Street that year? Why should the preservation of nineteenth-century buildings depend on deals improvised by the planners? Should City Hall officials and developers decide that a new park or museum will come into being?

In the 1990s no one can look back on the Bonus Era and declare it a total success, but it wasn't a failure either. On the one hand, about 6,000 units of social housing were built, parks were created, and some valuable historic architecture was partially saved, in the form of old facades shored up by new buildings placed behind them. On the other, bonusing pro-duced grotesque anomalies. Cadillac Fairview preserved, at great cost, the 1930s Toronto Stock Exchange on Bay Street, but wrapped it in a steel-and-glass, Mies-style office tower, creat-ing a jarringly contradictory facade that no one untutored in the ways of bonusing will ever understand. Stranger still, the old building became the Design Exchange, devoted to principles that its facade flagrantly violated. The exterior should have a plaque – IN MEMORIAM, THE BONUS ERA, 1982-88 – and a detail-ed explanation. Otherwise, future generations will imagine that designers of the 1990s were subject to fits of aesthetic madness.

Not far away, BCE Place, running from Bay to Yonge between Front and Wellington, tells another story. With its nobly soaring atrium designed by the Spanish engineer Santiago Calatrava, it stands as an elegant monument to the Bonus Era. The developers won the right to build it by providing a combination of social housing, workplace daycare, and heritage preservation. From almost anyone's point of view, BCE Place looked at the beginning like a success. It was only later that the owners discovered they couldn't rent it at the prices they expected to charge.

And then there was the vexed question of the Bay-Adelaide Centre.

THERE ARE MOMENTS in history when everyone has a confident opinion about events but no one truly knows what is happening. During the Toronto election campaign of November, 1988, when the Bay-Adelaide Centre became the focus of angry debate, no one imagined what was in store for the office-rental market. Consequently, no one understood that the political noise generated by Bay-Adelaide was the sound of an era ending.

Nor did anyone except a few planners, politicians, and developers entirely understand the deal. Ordinary newspaper readers probably saw Bay-Adelaide as another act in the long-running City Hall melodrama involving the pro-development forces on city council and their enemies, the reformers. The last meeting of the pre-election council heightened the theatricality by approving the Bay-Adelaide agreement, with its basket of bonuses for the developers and gifts for the city, at three o'clock in the morning. It looked to many like a victory for the rich and powerful, a defeat for those who wanted a more humane and livable city. The fact that it became law in the dark of night put a potent metaphor in the hands of those who opposed it.

A bitter struggle followed. Jack Layton, preparing for what turned out to be an unsuccessful campaign for mayor in 1991, denounced the deal. Reformers laid down a party line. Two New Democrats who broke ranks and supported Bay-Adelaide were later accused by Colin Vaughan – the Citytv political commentator and one-time reform alderman – of the crime of "ideological backsliding."

To those who voted on the reform side in the election, the moral was familiar. Yet again the city had made unconscionable allowances for a big developer, so that more gigantic towers could be jammed into the city core. And what had we received in return? Precious little, apparently. We had sold our heritage for (in a phrase popular among aldermen when I covered City Hall for *The Globe and Mail* in the 1950s) a mess of pottage.

Partly because of the furor over Bay-Adelaide, the reformers won the 1988 election and took control of council. It seemed that a new day had dawned at City Hall. The newspapers began speculating on how the reformers would use their power. Bay-Adelaide was now on the books, and the reformers had made it plain that they regarded this entire project as an effrontery. Could council reopen negotiations, perhaps retract the agreement that the 1988 council had (it was a legend now) slipped through in the post-midnight hours, when honest folk were home in their beds?

It wouldn't be easy. The late William Kilbourn, the historian and former alderman, pointed out that the city's chief planner, Robert Millward, had defended the deal in a letter to the editor of the Toronto *Star,* putting his department publicly on the record. This left the reformers on council in an uncomfortable position. If they wanted to argue against Bay-Adelaide and ask the Ontario Municipal Board to overturn the 1988 decision, they would have to hire outside consultants to fight the position of their own planning department.

Council instead commissioned a study from Hemson Consulting. After half a dozen planners, a transportation expert, and a firm of lawyers examined the deal and worked out the costs, Hemson came back with a surprising conclusion: it was a bargain for the city. To get increased allowances worth something under $75 million, the developers were paying about $80 million in the form of a park, housing, the preservation of heritage buildings, and other benefits. In Hemson's view, the deal-making process had been flawed, but the result was good. "The city obtained substantial benefits for comparatively small costs while the developer paid a substantial price for benefits received." At City Hall, talk of reopening Bay-Adelaide quietly died.

Soon the market for office space also began to die. Every day it became clearer that there were more offices than tenants. Rents began falling, and each lease that came up for renewal was rewritten at a lower figure, thereby lowering the potential value of future buildings, like the Bay-Adelaide Centre. It became obvious to Markborough and Trizec that the concessions they had won were, at least for the moment, worth nothing. In fact, they were worth less than nothing, since the Bay-Adelaide Centre had to be stopped in its tracks. The developers put a two-year hold on it, extended that for about eight months, and then stopped talking about it entirely. It appeared unlikely to be built before the twenty-first century. Yet the developers had to make good on their promises to the city. The social-housing benefits were handed over and the park was finished. The city came out, for the foreseeable future, some $80 million ahead.

While discussing the Bonus Era with planners at City Hall, I expressed astonishment at this outcome. The planners, if they were once surprised, didn't show it. They calmly explained that, following normal practice, the developers had handed over the package of benefits before receiving their building permit. They had not asked for a change in the agreement, and in any case there was no way to give them one. It was part of their cost of doing business.

By then, the bizarre ironies of the Bonus Era were obvious – and so was the most unhappy aspect of bonusing. On the psychological level, it erodes the political culture. It produces civic discomfort because it encourages the belief that the city's fate is being decided in secret by a few dozen technocrats and billionaires. There's something disquietingly primitive about it, as there is about most forms of bartering. This sometimes clumsy system seems an odd way for Toronto to have developed much of its highly sophisticated financial district. What seems stranger still is that, in the case of Bay-Adelaide, the Bonus Era left behind something that looked remarkably like a masterpiece.

It was certainly among the most impressive architectural accomplishments of the 1990s. Unexpectedly appearing at the core of the business district, filling a half-acre site between Richmond Street and Temperance Street, Bay-Adelaide Park seems even more remarkable in Toronto than it might in another city. Our downtown parks have traditionally been few in number and meanly designed, as if calculated to show that the Toronto civic imagination is stunted. Bay-Adelaide Park refutes that bleak history. It's everything our parks have never been, a powerful public space that combines audacious theory and populist images, a place we can enjoy immediately and savour for many years. The fact that this $5 million architectural fantasy could only have been built as a gift from property developers – no city government would spend so much on so small a space – intensifies the irony.

Looming over the park, six stories high and pathetic in its raw concrete nakedness, is the beginning of what would have been the service core of the centre's fifty-seven-storey tower. This blue-gray stump, looking like a rough abstract sculpture magnified several hundred times, is the remnant of what was not built, a monument to intoxicated dreams. Christopher Hume in the *Star* named it the Magnificent Hulk, "an instant ruin, engineered to withstand the vicissitudes of everything but recessionary economics"; unlike most ruins, it's "a testament not to what was but to what might have been, all the more moving for its accidental genesis." It's a bizarre element in the cityscape, a reminder that the park was to have been the last element of the centre completed but turned out to be the first – and, for now, the only one.

In a curious way, the raw service tower fits the mood of the place. It needs only some hanging vines to make us think of the glory that was Rome. As it happens, the ruins of old cities in Europe were among the inspirations for the park's design. George Baird and Barry Sampson, the architects who won the design competition, and Margaret Priest, the artist who designed the wall sculpture on the east side, began formulating their ideas by thinking about the value that civilization has traditionally given to ruins.

Their design emerged out of a self-conscious view of cultural history. When they began planning the submission that won the contest, they talked about a structure that would carry meaning as well as provide pleasure; they hoped to say something memorable about Toronto. Baird, in a 1981 essay, wrote that Toronto architecture should articulate symbols representing the aspirations of its citizens. He said this was architecture's most crucial role in human history and "the most difficult task facing contemporary architects." Baird and Sampson saw Bay-Adelaide as a chance to make a place richly layered with meaning.

Approaching their task, they looked at the work of Giovanni Battista Piranesi, the eighteenth-century artist whose 1,500 etchings and drawings became part of the standard repertoire of images lodged in the western imagination. Piranesi's accomplishment was unique and permanent: he taught Europeans to appreciate the poignant beauty of ancient buildings in a state of decay. A Piranesi etching of the Roman Forum, for instance, shows trees growing out of the roofs of temples and the ground creeping halfway up the ancient columns. He evokes a melancholy reflection on time and history. In Piranesi's day, ruins became so well loved that they were often created artificially. They gave a picturesque and history-laden quality to the gardens of great families, and offered a pious reminder that wealth and power inevitably decay.

Well before the ruined dreams of developers gave this theme powerful resonance in Toronto, Baird and Sampson decided that a park embodying some of Piranesi's themes could stand as a metaphor of urban development. A city, after all, is at any moment both a construction project and a ruin; when something is built, something is destroyed. In a city that's normally averse to monuments, they decided to make a monument to city-building itself, to the idea of a city as eternally a work in progress.

On the subject of ruins, Margaret Priest is a romantic. She lovingly remembers her intense feelings when she read, as a child in London, about a Roman temple uncovered by excavations for the Underground. It excited her to know she was living, literally, on top of the ancient world. After she moved to Toronto she worked with Baird-Sampson on an unsuccessful proposal for the Trinity Square Park beside the Eaton Centre. When they began preparing for the Bay-Adelaide competition they asked Priest and her husband, the artist Tony Scherman, to contribute ideas.

Priest's own drawings were once described as "cooled-out Piranesi." She quickened to the notion of ruins as an element of design. "There were no ruins in Toronto," she has explained. "All of us spoke about the role of ruins in major cities – the ruins in Rome, for instance. We decided we would have a ruin in this park – but it would have to be a modernist ruin."

Eventually the design team arrived at a plan in which trees are rooted above ground level, as Piranesi found them in Rome, and vines creep inexorably over stones. They devised a modernist steel structure on which they could hang these elements, as paintings are hung in art galleries; in places it would look half-finished, like the bare steel frames city-dwellers are accustomed to seeing as buildings go up. They also built massive retaining walls with – as George Kapelos explained when showing drawings of their work in a 1994 exhibition at the McMichael Gallery – "lush ground level plantings, reminiscent of successive abandoned foundations." As Kapelos wrote, "Throughout the park, walls and other large blocks appear as incidents of construction, disassembly and ruin. Similarly, rough, stratified limestone bands allude to the sedimentary layers embedded in the natural history of the stone quarry and of the city."

Baird and Sampson also drew inspiration from the nineteenth-century Parc des Buttes Chaumont in northeast Paris, which inserts into the urban fabric a suspension bridge, a mountain, and miniature gorges. Using the exposed-steel language of modernism, Baird and Sampson built an observation platform and a roaring waterfall – a condensed, melodramatic version of natural landscape. They built it vertically, as if the trees and shrubs were reaching for sunlight, and stacked it in a style that echoes the Acropolis and other monuments of antiquity. You don't just visit the Bay-Adelaide Park, you ascend it. At the top they erected a greenhouse, which in wintry Toronto feels like a fantasy version of the tropics. Their park resembles a poem that makes a strong first impression and then reveals more layers of meaning each time we return to it.

The call for entries in the competition suggested that the park include a monument to construction workers. In the Baird-Sampson proposal, this took the form of a gigantic sculpture covering much of the east wall, twenty-two metres wide, ten metres high. It became Margaret Priest's responsibility, and she brought to it an unusual mixture of sensibilities: she's a middle-class university professor, now living in Forest Hill, who grew up in an English working-class family dominated by railroad men and construction workers. Her childhood left her with a reverence for the work of artisans. She remembers her father describing a certain locomotive as "exquisite" and an uncle calling the wall of a nineteenth-century cathedral a "bloody marvelous bit of mortar." She decided the monument to construction workers would not depict workers ("I didn't want a bloke with a hammer in his pocket") but would focus on their accomplishments instead. It would be executed by the skilled workers of Toronto themselves – glaziers, pipe fitters, sheet metal workers, sprinkler fitters, refrigeration workers, and many other trades. It would be a way that future generations could appreciate these crafts. In Priest's mind, the finely detailed work that normally goes unnoticed became the point of the piece. She would honour the building trades by placing their work in an outdoor museum.

Priest especially wanted to reveal the inner life of buildings and celebrate the hidden skills of workers who create the labyrinth of wires, pipes, and steel beneath the surface of construction. The below-grade floors of the Bay-Adelaide Centre were being built as she prepared her design. Priest climbed through them, examining the details of construction and searching for shapes she could use. She learned that some of her preconceptions about building were outdated. She assumed, for instance, that rivets would be part of the design. "They hooted with laughter. I might as well have talked about thatching." Rivets, apparently, belong to yesterday.

She designed the mural as fifty-nine rust-coloured steel panels spread against the east wall. She filled twenty-five of them with abstract designs representing construction trades, put blank concrete in twenty-four other panels, and left eleven of them empty. The eleven openings allow us to look through the mural as well as at it. What we see behind it is a blank wall that was not built to be seen but was exposed when the building on the park's site was demolished; Priest liked "the Dickensian picturesqueness of the old wall," with its sloppy mortar.

One of the squares in the finished work is a design of rebars, the rods that reinforce concrete. The craft of the sprinkler fitters is represented by a design of pipes. There's a square filled with intricately crafted wood joints, another formed from soldered copper sheet, another from glazed glass. Priest can describe the meaning of each square with passion. Of a ridged-concrete square that looks like a Constructivist painting from 1920s Moscow, she says: "If you know anything about concrete, that workmanship is a joy to behold – it requires immensely skilled carpentry [to make the wooden form] and immensely skilled pouring."

She found the workers careful, thoughtful, and anxious to make a monument that would represent them honestly. They were not always uncritical of her ideas. "The electricians are a difficult lot," Priest says. They made valid objections to her working drawings and she redesigned their square three times, until it made sense to them. Behind all this activity was another level of irony: having been prevented by the recession from doing the work they expected to do at Bay-Adelaide, the workers were nevertheless enlisted in the making of a monument to commemorate precisely that work.

Priest took special care with the plaque that explains the wall. Gary Michael Dault wrote the text, with a little help from Liz Braun and Constance Rooke. The result is the only Toronto plaque I've ever read that conveys nobility of purpose: "...Here, laid bare and presented in a new context, is the raw stuff of building, a vertical tray of samples crafted and erected by construction workers....A gallery for the framing of building blocks and construction procedures, the Monument to Construction Workers is offered in homage to the workers.... It is a testament to their courage and perseverance in the face of bodily risk...."

The Bay-Adelaide Park was supposed to be squeezed between giant buildings, as if something brutal, powerful, and organic were emerging from the ground. It was meant to symbolize nature in contrast with advanced commercial culture. Instead, it exists in the face of a gigantic absence, and feels less intense and dramatic than it should. It's a picture that lacks a proper frame. Even so, it's a magnificent picture.

BAY-ADELAIDE IS the most striking development in a largely unnoticed change in Toronto, the appearance of a network of fifteen downtown parks. As recently as the 1970s, public open spaces were few. The downtown parks consisted mainly of historic remnants, like Queen's Park, the lawn in front of Osgoode Hall, and Grange Park. For generations, the creation of downtown parks failed to appear on the city's agenda. In fact, no new park was created between the First World War and very recent times. Even in the relatively rich 1950s and 1960s, most of the parks department budget went into swimming pools and other recreational facilities across the city.

As buildings grew taller, the need for parks in the core of the city became obvious, and the popularity of Nathan Phillips Square implied that they should be a natural part of modern Toronto. But there was no money for them and no reason to believe money would ever appear. That's why the Central Area Plan of 1976 proposed that the city acquire parkland through development bonuses and the swapping of city-owned land and road allowances. Miraculously, this system worked. It created everything from the large Harbour Square lands to the minuscule McGill Parkette at 415 Yonge, from the tiny Isabella Valancy Crawford Park beside the CN Tower to the elaborate and well used Village of Yorkville Park, with its gigantic chunk of the Canadian Shield, its impressive plantings, and a wall of water that imitates rainfall in summer and turns to icicles in winter.

In this process, the ironies of the Bay-Adelaide experience were not unique. Both College Park, on Yonge south of College Street, and Trinity Square, behind the Eaton Centre, are gifts from developers who still haven't exercised all the development rights they acquired years ago by providing the parks. These parks at street level also function as the roofs of the underground city: Trinity Square rests on a truck ramp and part of a hotel, Bay-Adelaide on top of a parking garage and unused retail space.

Whatever the compromises and disappointments that lie behind them, the new downtown parks together make up one of the great successes of recent Toronto city-building. Their number continues to grow. As this book was being finished, so were new downtown parks: Courthouse Square, to the west of St. James Cathedral, and a new park on the west side of Jarvis Street, south of the St. Lawrence Market, were being prepared. Simcoe Place Park, next to the CBC building, was all but open.

The story of these parks, their evolution and their appearance as part of the city, parallels the story that Bay-Adelaide tells about Toronto through symbols. When all the work on that monument was completed, when every panel was bolted on and every stone fixed in place, Margaret Priest's mother asked her, "When will it be finished, dear?" As with the city itself, the answer, of course, is never.

Bibliography

Ardiel, June. *Sculpture/Toronto: An Illustrated Guide to Toronto's Historic and Contemporary Sculpture.* Toronto: Leidra Books, 1994.

Arthur, Eric. *Toronto, No Mean City,* rev. ed. Toronto: University of Toronto Press, 1974.

Atwood, Margaret. *The Robber Bride.* Toronto: McClelland & Stewart, 1993.

Baird, George, and Mark Lewis. *Queues, Rendezvous, Riots: Questioning the Public in Art and Architecture.* Banff: Walter Philips Gallery, 1994.

Baraness, Marc, and Larry Richards, eds. *Toronto Places: A Context for Urban Design.* Toronto: City of Toronto and University of Toronto Press, 1992.

Berman, Marshall. *All That Is Solid Melts Into Air.* New York: Simon and Schuster, 1982.

Bernstein, William, and Ruth Cawker, eds. *Building with Words: Canadian Architects on Architecture.* Toronto: Coach House Press, 1981.

Bernstein, William, and Ruth Cawker. *Contemporary Canadian*

Architecture: The Mainstream and Beyond. Toronto: Fitzhenry & Whiteside, 1982.

Blake, Peter. *No Place Like Utopia: Modern Architecture and the Company We Kept.* New York: Knopf 1993.

Boyer, Barbara. *The Boardwalk Album: Memories of The Beach.* Erin, Ontario: Boston Mills Press, 1985.

Bush, Catherine. *Minus Time.* Toronto: HarperCollins, 1993.

Campbell, Mary, and Barbara Myrvold. *The Beach in Pictures, 1793-1932.* Toronto: Toronto Public Library, 1988.

Caulfield, Jon. *The Tiny Perfect Mayor: David Crombie and Toronto's reform aldermen.* Toronto: J. Lorimer, 1974.

Charlesworth, Hector. *Candid Chronicles.* Toronto: Macmillan of Canada, 1925.

Coldwell, Joan, ed. *The Tightrope Walker: Autobiographical Writings of Anne Wilkinson.* Toronto: University of Toronto Press, 1992.

Colton, Timothy J. *Big Daddy: Frederick G. Gardiner and the Building of Metropolitan Toronto.* Toronto: University of Toronto Press, 1980.

Crombie, David, et al., eds. *Regeneration: Toronto's waterfront and the sustainable city: final report.* Toronto: Royal Commission on the Future of the Toronto Waterfront, 1992.

Dale, John R., *Barton Myers: Selected and Current Works.* Mulgrave, Australia: Images Publishing Group, 1994.

Davies, Robertson. *The Cunning Man.* Toronto: McClelland & Stewart, 1994.

Dendy, William. *Lost Toronto.* Toronto: Oxford University Press, 1978.

Dendy, William, and William Kilbourn. *Toronto Observed: Its Architecture, Patrons, and History*. Toronto: Oxford University Press, 1986.

du Toit, Roger, et al. *The Art of the Avenue: A University Avenue Public Art Study*. Toronto: du Toit, Allsopp, Hillier, 1989.

Firth, Edith G. *Toronto in Art: 150 Years Through Artists' Eyes*. Toronto: Fitzhenry & Whiteside in association with the City of Toronto, 1983.

Firth, Edith G., ed. *The Town of York, 1793-1815, A Collection of Documents of Early Toronto*. Toronto: Champlain Society for the Government of Ontario, 1962.

Fram, Mark. *Toronto, and beyond: the Society for Industrial Archeology Conference Guidebook*. Toronto: Society for Industrial Archeology, 1984.

Freedman, Adele. *Sight Lines: Looking at architecture and design in Canada*. Toronto: Oxford University Press, 1990.

Gibson, Sally. *More Than an Island: A History of the Toronto Island*. Toronto: Irwin, 1984.

Grant, James. *Money of the Mind: Borrowing and Lending in America from the Civil War to Michael Milken*. New York: Farrar, Straus & Giroux, 1992.

Gratz, Roberta Brandes. *The Living City,* rev. ed. Washington: Simon and Schuster, 1989.

Heidegger, Martin. *Basic Writings*. Edited by D. F. Krell. New York: HarperCollins Publishers, 1993.

Hood, Hugh. *The Governor's Bridge is Closed*. Ottawa: Oberon Press, 1973.

Hough, Michael. *Out of Place: Restoring Identity to the Regional Landscape*. New Haven: Yale University Press, 1990.

Hughes, Robert. *The Shock of the New*. London: Alfred A. Knopf, 1980.

Jackson, A. Y. *A Painter's Country*. Toronto: Clarke Irwin, 1964.

Jacobs, Jane. *The Death and Life of Great American Cities*. New York: Random House, 1961.

Kalman, Harold. *A History of Canadian Architecture*. 2 vols. Toronto: Oxford University Press, 1994.

Kapelos, George Thomas. *Interpretations of Nature: Contemporary Canadian Architecture, Landscape, and Urbanism*. Toronto: McMichael Canadian Art Collection, 1994.

Kilbourn, William. *Toronto Remembered: A Celebration of the City*. Toronto: Stoddart, 1984.

Levitt, Cyril, and William Shaffir. *The Riot at Christie Pits*. Toronto: Lester & Orpen Dennys, 1987.

Litvak, Marilyn. *The Grange: A Gentleman's House in Upper Canada*. Toronto: Art Gallery of Ontario, 1988.

Lownsbrough, John. *The Privileged Few: The Grange & Its People in Nineteenth Century Toronto*, with an essay on restoration by Peter John Stokes and "The Alienation of the Grange Property," by John Coleman. Toronto: Art Gallery of Ontario, 1980.

Mays, John Bentley. *Emerald City: Toronto Visited*. Toronto: Viking, 1994.

McHugh, Patricia. *Toronto Architecture: A City Guide*. Toronto: Mercury Books, 1985.

Mertins, Detlef, ed. *The Presence of Mies.* New York: Princeton Architectural Press, 1994.

Mertins, Detlef, ed. *Metropolitan Mutations: The Architecture of Emerging Public Spaces.* Boston: Little, Brown, 1989.

Miller, Donald L. *Lewis Mumford: A Life.* New York: Weidenfeld & Nicolson, 1989.

Ondaatje, Michael. *In the Skin of a Lion.* Toronto: McClelland & Stewart, 1987.

Parkin, Jeanne. *Art in Architecture.* Toronto: Visual Arts Ontario, 1982.

Parkinson, C. Northcote. *Parkinson's Law.* Boston: Houghton Mifflin, 1957.

Proulx, E. Annie. *The Shipping News.* New York: Scribner, 1993.

Poulton, Ron. *The Paper Tyrant: John Ross Robertson of the Toronto Telegram.* Toronto: Clarke, Irwin, 1971.

Reid, Dennis. *The Group of Seven.* Ottawa: National Gallery of Canada, 1970.

Relph, Edward. *The Toronto Guide: the City, Metro, the Region.* Toronto: Association of American Geographers, 1990.

Riddell, W. R. *The Life of John Graves Simcoe.* Toronto: McClelland & Stewart, 1926.

Sewell, John. *The Shape of the City: Toronto Struggles with Modern Planning.* Toronto: University of Toronto Press, 1993.

Sewell, John. *Up Against City Hall.* Toronto: James, Lewis & Samuel, 1972.

Sherlock, Harley. *Cities Are Good For Us*. London: Paladin, 1991.

Smith, Goldwin. *Reminiscences*. New York: Macmillan Co., 1911.

Taylor, Charles. *Radical Tories: The Conservative Tradition in Canada*. Toronto: House of Anansi Press, 1982.

Wilkinson, Alan. *Henry Moore Remembered*. Toronto: Key Porter Books, 1987.

Wilkinson, Alan. *The Moore Collection in the Art Gallery of Ontario*. Toronto: Art Gallery of Ontario, 1979.

Withrow, William, et al. *Art Gallery of Ontario: Selected Works*. Toronto: Art Gallery of Ontario, 1990.

Acknowledgments

Geraldine Sherman, my wife, read this book in many versions and provided, as always, perceptive and imaginative criticism. Gary Ross proved, as he has so often before, a skillful and sensitive editor. Sara Borins's expert copy editing saved me from many gaucheries. My agent, Beverley Slopen, steered the manuscript toward precisely the right publishers. Diane Gee, my researcher for a quarter of a century, carved a path through the factual history of Toronto. James, Margaret, Rachel and Sarah Fulford helped me in many ways, often by specific intent and often through their spontaneous observations. Wayne Fulford shared his perceptions of Scarborough. June Ardiel, Helen Juhola, Joan Murray, and Alan Wilkinson provided helpful comments on individual chapters. As a reader of this book will understand, much of it is written under the influence of, and out of gratitude for, the work of Jane Jacobs.

Some of the material in this book appeared, in earlier versions, in *Toronto Life*, and in *Américas*, *Canadian Art*, *Canadian Geographic*, the Chicago *Tribune*, *Country Estate*, *The Globe and Mail*, *Insite*, *The Imperial Oil Review*, *The New York Times Book Review*, the Toronto *Star*, *Saturday Night*, and *Venue*. I'm grateful to all the editors who have given a home to my ideas, and in particular to Angie Gardos and John Macfarlane at *Toronto Life* and Sarah Milroy at *Canadian Art*.

Index

Design by Hahn Smith Design

Map by J. Loates, Visutronx

Typeset by Tony Gordon/Image One Ltd.

This book is set in Sabon and Din.
Sabon was originally cut in 1532 by
Claude Garamond, a punch cutter in
Paris, and was updated in 1968
by Jan Tschichold. Din was designed in
postwar Germany, as a typeface for
road signs. Din is the abbreviation
for Deutsches Institut Für Normung,
the German Institute for Standards.